CHESTERFIELD *County* CHRONICLES

CHESTERFIELD
• County •
CHRONICLES

Stories from the James to the Appomattox

Diane C. Dallmeyer

THE History PRESS

Published by The History Press
Charleston, SC 29403
www.historypress.net

Cover images: 1917 courthouse. *Courtesy George Cranford*; Beaufont Springs. *Courtesy Page Dowdy*; Pocahontas, oil on tapestry, artist Mary Ellen Howe; image of tree taken by author.

First published 2011

Manufactured in the United States

ISBN 978.1.60949.142.0

Dallmeyer, Diane C.
Chesterfield County chronicles : stories from the James to the Appomattox / Diane C. Dallmeyer.
p. cm.
Includes bibliographical references and index.
ISBN 978-1-60949-142-0
1. Chesterfield County (Va.)--History. 2. Chesterfield County (Va.)--History, Local. 3. Chesterfield County (Va.)--Biography. I. Title.
F232.C52D35 2011
975.5'594--dc22
2011012907

Notice: The information in this book is true and complete to the best of our knowledge. It is offered without guarantee on the part of the author or The History Press. The author and The History Press disclaim all liability in connection with the use of this book.

For my father, Larry Cripe, who taught me to love and respect the power and beauty of the written word. I miss you, Dad.

Contents

Foreword

"You can't see the forest for the trees!" This old chestnut means that the real truth is in the "big picture" and that if you want to learn something, don't focus on the details. Growing up, I always questioned it, thinking that if you didn't know anything about trees, how can you even begin to understand the forest?

I found that this adage guides the way we learned history in school—Columbus discovered America, George Washington freed the nation, Abraham Lincoln freed the slaves and so on. But did you ever learn the names of any of Washington's soldiers or of even a single slave? I know I didn't. To understand the American West, you studied Manifest Destiny. Of course, you never learned the names of any of these pioneers. But that's okay—the big sweep of history just doesn't have a place for the common man or woman. You can take all of the history classes you can sign up for, and you will never learn anything about your great-great-grandparents or what was going on in your neighborhood one hundred years ago.

But local history turns this approach on its ear. It's about the details. It's about your family and your community. It's about stories passed down from generation to generation or derived by researchers today looking at old documents and piecing together what life might have been like.

If you live in Chesterfield County, count yourself lucky as far as local history goes. First, it goes back more than four hundred years. That's a long time. If your ancestors were early settlers of Bermuda Hundred, they could well be your fifteenth great-grandparents. And the county is big. It is nearly five hundred square miles. That's why those of French ancestry (the

Huguenots) could live on one side, and the English on the other side were okay with that. One part of the county (Manchester) was completely urban, while others were pure wilderness.

So the county is a great stage for local history. There is just one piece missing. You can't have a story without a storyteller. The Chesterfield Historical Society of Virginia has been researching the history of this county for thirty years. If you have ever visited a historical society—there are thousands of them across the country—you will find them full of filing cabinets packed with documents and research, books, old maps and artifacts from the past.

In Chesterfield, all of this was just waiting for a storyteller to come in and breathe new life into the research that so many had labored to put together. And we found just the person. A few years ago, we were lucky to have Diane Dallmeyer come to work with us. Soon after, the stories started to flow, and the research that was so carefully done was liberated so that it could be understood and enjoyed by everyone.

So if you like trees, and I have never met anyone who doesn't, you will like this book.

Peter Lipowicz
Former President
Chesterfield Historical Society of Virginia

Introduction

It's not history, it's storytelling! One of the best parts of working for the Chesterfield Historical Society of Virginia is watching young children's eyes grow wide when they participate in the *Then and Now* program at Magnolia Grange plantation house and discover how Victorian women curled their hair or what colonial children did for fun. How contagious is the enthusiasm of three teenage girls in the library researching haunted houses. How stirring is the solemn soldier reenactment by young boys with Revolutionary wooden muskets play "drilling" on the Courthouse Green.

These young people forget that it's history. Imagination takes hold as they realize for the first time that kids just like them for generations have called Chesterfield home, and they become entranced with the stories of how those children lived.

Remember, before history began to be recorded, it was passed down by oral tradition, and the excitement of those stories stirred generation after generation. It's the same today; the years have gone, but the stories bear striking resemblances to those of our twenty-first-century world: babies are born out of wedlock, people hurt and kill others, couples who shouldn't marry do (and those who should don't), families move away to explore new frontiers and new adventures and folks respond to tragedies with courage and passion. The difference in the "old" stories is that they portray the events and the people who shaped the communities that we know today. Look at a current map of Chesterfield County, and you'll see the index of our county's history in the names of the streets, subdivisions and schools we see daily.

I invite you to read the stories. I encourage you to *tell* them, to your children and to your friends. I challenge you to find other stories. Chesterfield has a few hundred years' worth of stories to tell! In the meantime, get your feet wet with the stories that follow and let your imagination take root. Consider this: remembering our past is our obligation to the future.

Chesterfield is endowed by the scholarship of historians such as Bettie Woodson Weaver, Jeffrey O'Dell and Francis Lutz. Their books are the foundation on which many of these stories have been built. Your exploration of your county's history ought to start with one of these fine works, which are available in the county library system, the county schools and available for sale in the Magnolia Grange gift shop.

Special thanks and appreciation go to the dedicated and impassioned volunteers with the Chesterfield Historical Society of Virginia for igniting in me an unsuspected zeal for story collecting. To society president Liess van der Linden-Brusse and Peter and Rachel Lipowicz, I say that this storyteller is grateful to you.

Part I
WHO WE ARE

Eighty miles up our river from Jamestown I have surveyed a convenient, strong, healthie and sweete site to plant a new towne.

—*Sir Thomas Dale*

Indian tribes once flourished along the banks of the James and Appomattox Rivers, including the Powhatan tribe of the Indian princess Pocahontas. Mere days after arriving in Jamestown, our early colonists boated up the James and scouted the area later called Bermuda Hundred in Chesterfield County. The decision to settle downriver in Jamestown shaped history, although the location proved to be a poor choice. Weather, disease and famine were the terrible hardships endured in the early years, and in 1610, Sir Thomas Dale went looking for a better place to build an English settlement.

The city of Henricus was founded in 1611 and named for Henry, Prince of Wales. The Virginia Company of London intended it to be a replacement for the unhealthy Jamestown. In this area in 1612, tobacco was cultivated successfully, finally providing the London Company with a sound economic basis for continuing to support its thus unprofitable venture in the New World. Bermuda Hundred was incorporated as the first town in America, and the first land grants were awarded here, providing the first private ownership of land in this country.

By 1619, settlers had moved up the river closer to the center of Chesterfield and established the first iron furnace. March 22, 1622, brought a massive, well-planned attack by Indians that covered the area from the Falls to Jamestown and tragically put an end to this endeavor before it was able to produce goods for the London Company. In 1701, coal was found in the Midlothian region of Chesterfield and was moved along the first railroad, a gravity-fed line going downhill to the James. The coal was sent back to England—the first commercially mined coal in America.

Previously part of the sprawling Henrico County, Chesterfield was officially established in 1749 by the British House of Burgesses and presumably named for Philip Dormer Stanhope, Earl of Chesterfield, a British statesman. Later, Chesterfield served as a supply depot and training center for soldiers in the American Revolution.

During the Civil War, crucial supplies were brought to Richmond through Chesterfield's system of railroads. That railroad system, along with the bordering James and Appomattox Rivers, as well as its proximity to Richmond, the capital of the Confederacy, ensured Chesterfield a central role in the war effort. Many key battles were fought in the Chesterfield area, and General Robert E. Lee stayed with Chesterfield residents as he made his sad journey to surrender at Appomattox in 1865.

Now the third-largest county in Virginia, Chesterfield is home to more than 316,000 residents, as well as a large variety of business and industry.

WHY ARE WE CALLED CHESTERFIELD?

Contrary to the belief that Chesterfield was named after a cigarette, in reality our county was most likely named for an earl, an English nobleman named Philip Dormer Stanhope, born in London in September 1694. The son of an aristocratic couple, Philip lost his mother early in his childhood. His maternal grandparents took the young boy in, and their raising of him, along with being a part of the society in which they lived, influenced Philip as a boy and into manhood. His grandfather and his father, the latter particularly known as a hothead, held opposing political views, and it was best that they not spend much time in each other's company. It seems that Philip inherited little from his father other than his short stature, while the grandparents provided him with a private classical education and the social company of boys from similar backgrounds. Philip's lifelong habit of rising early and striving to be productive was due to the influence of his grandparents, as was his pastime of writing letters—his grandfather was a prolific writer who wrote a book called *Advice to a Daughter* along with autobiographical and political tracts.

Philip is reported to have been passionate, engaging and active in his youth. It is recorded that he had so upset and disappointed himself with something he said as a temperamental young man that he vowed to exert better control of his tongue, a characteristic that served him well in his later years. He seemed to have determined to become a statesman by the time he arrived at Cambridge in 1712 at the age of eighteen. He considered himself a Whig (mainly upper class and liberal-leaning) and spent his college days arguing politics and behaving as university students did in that time (as well as today). He was a disciplined student but left Cambridge after a year to travel abroad and gain some social polish. He spent time at the Hague and in Belgium, where he picked up a bad habit he was never entirely able to break: gambling.

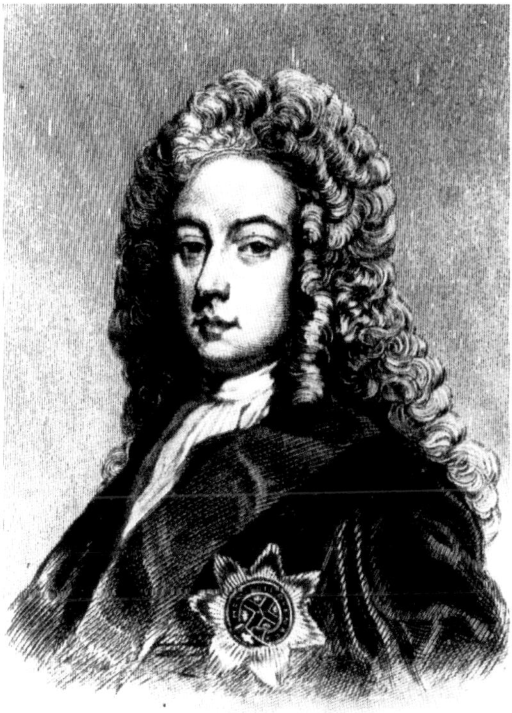

Philip Dormer Stanhope, fourth Earl of Chesterfield, as a young man. *Chesterfield Historical Society of Virginia.*

An Ambitious Young Man

Philip was an astute observer of human nature and social propriety and seemed to be determined to fashion himself as he thought he should be rather than as the shy and unattractive person he was by nature. Because he was likeable, he found strong mentors in the high society of France, where he lived briefly after leaving Cambridge. Philip entered the British House of Commons in 1715 and fulfilled his ambitious plan of becoming Somebody Important. He gave his first speech in Parliament only to be reprimanded by a member of the opposing Tory party that he was underage and could be fined if he dared to cast a vote.

He left Parliament for a brief time and became an attendant to the Prince of Wales, a position he secured through the influence of his father. Politics in England at this time was in turmoil, and Chesterfield was careful about whom he aligned himself with. He wanted to shine, to be in the right circles at the right time, but his physical appearance worked against him. Short, with badly stained teeth and an unappealing voice, he was often considered too fawning or eager to please. But he had a sharp wit and a sense of satire that entertained as many people as it offended. King George II called him a "dwarf baboon." In later life, Philip would write, "Wit is so shining a quality, that everybody admires it, most people aim at it, all people fear it, and few love it unless in themselves…The more wit you have, the more good-nature and politeness you must show."

In 1725, his father became seriously ill and called Philip to look after him. Philip considered this punishment and wrote, "Had I been a Papist (as, thank God, I am not), I should have thought myself in purgatory; but, being a good Protestant, I am obliged most orthodoxly to conclude myself to be in Hell." Unfortunately, the lack of a relationship with the father who had left him to his in-laws' upbringing made this time in Philip Stanhope's life unbearable, and he was plainly relieved when his father died and he was able to escape his duties while assuming the title and his father's place in the Upper House. In 1728, he was sent to Holland as an ambassador.

Middle Years

Philip Stanhope didn't marry until he was about forty, and his marriage to the Countess of Walsingham seemed to have been a good match for both: he gained some financial advantage and she gained a social position. He wrote, "There are but two objects in marriage; love or money. If you marry for love, you will certainly have some very happy days and probably many very uneasy ones; if for money, you will have no happy days and probably no uneasy ones: in this latter case let the woman at least be such a one that you can live decently and amicably with." Although he had good female friends, Philip's opinion of women was true to his day; he told his son that women were but children of a larger growth, yet they were useful to teach you manners—they had a sense of such things—and you might chatter agreeably with them.

Philip remained involved in the many twists and turns of power and politics in England for twenty years. Maintaining his independence was important to him, and this independence probably kept him from being more politically successful. He was not a polished leader and didn't naturally possess a silver tongue, but he prepared himself thoroughly, did his research in preparing his commentaries and was considered a patriot and an orator. He spoke on the change from the Julian to the Gregorian calendar and on freedom of the press, and he began contributing pieces to periodicals.

Philip became Viceroy of Ireland in 1744 and secretary of state in 1746. In his retirement, he wrote, "I have time both to read and to think; the first I like, the latter I am not, as many are, afraid of."

A Man of Letters

Perhaps Philip Stanhope's best claim to immortality is found in his letters to his son. He wrote:

> *As fathers commonly go, it is seldom a misfortune to be fatherless; and, considering the general run of sons, as seldom a misfortune to be childless. You and I form, I believe, an exception to that rule; for I am persuaded that we would neither of us change our relation, were it in our power. You will, I both hope and believe, be not only the comfort but the pride of my age; and I am sure I will be the support, the friend, the guide of your youth. Trust me without reserve; I will advise you without private interest, or secret envy.*

Philip Stanhope's illegitimate son, Philip also, was thoroughly groomed by Lord Chesterfield to follow in his family footsteps into Parliament. Terribly shy, this was not to be. However, young Philip did secure a post in Germany and had a place in the diplomatic world. His son's failure to advance was very disappointing to Stanhope, and his death at a young age devastated him, particularly when Stanhope learned that his cherished son had secretly married a woman of a lower class and had two sons who were unknown to their grandfather. Never one to complain, Chesterfield graciously took his new family under his wing in England and began taking part in the education of his grandsons.

In the early 1760s, he adopted his godson and heir, also named Philip Stanhope. His later years were full of wit and serenity, and he was an old man who made the best of things. He continued to have strong opinions on religion and politics, as well as the upbringing of the young. At his death, he was known as a wit, a social figure and an honest statesman. Not a bad namesake for our county.

Visit Chesterfield's Center: The Historic Courthouse Green

Everywhere one turns in Chesterfield County, there are deep pockets of history. Bermuda Hundred was once a bustling seaport, and Midlothian and Winterpock had the first coal mines. On the river, Warwick was a tobacco port, and the northernmost part of the county featured premier granite quarries. Bon Air was the first resort town, and Falling Creek had the first ironworks. But it is at the heart of Chesterfield, in today's county administrative complex, where native and tourist can experience a microcosm of four hundred years of local history in one brief, relaxing stroll around the Courthouse Green, a designated district on the National Register of Historic Places that includes two landscaped acres, the 1917 courthouse, the 1892 jail and the 1828 and 1889 clerks' offices.

First There Was a Tavern

Not just anyone could open a tavern, or ordinary, in the early days of our county. A man had to apply, and the county officials had to ascertain that he was a man of good character, one who could keep things in his establishment under control, provide sufficient food and drink for travelers and their animals and manage the only legally sanctioned place where liquor could be sold to drink on site. Prices at the ordinary were regulated by the court. Ordinaries were situated on main thoroughfares and served as gathering places for neighbors, travelers and, in the case of the Courthouse Green, those involved in court affairs. John Howlett's Tavern, probably the first in the courthouse area, was located north of Swift Creek and south of Five Forks, the area where Newby's Bridge, Courthouse and Belmont Roads and Route 288 converge. It was probably at Howlett's that the county leaders first met to decide the location of the new courthouse. Undoubtedly, geography played the key role in this decision. Located centrally in the county and adjacent to a source of fresh water, Cold Water Run, several roads crossed here, making ease of transportation a deciding factor. Archaeological evidence shows that Native Americans also found the area a hospitable camping, hunting and farming area thousands of years before Europeans arrived at the same decision. We know from survey maps that the Courthouse Green was about two acres in 1814, the same as today, but it was likely about triple that size when established in 1749.

Buildings

The original Chesterfield Courthouse was built when Chesterfield was formed out of Henrico in 1749, and it was of like dimensions to the one in Henrico. The building was rectangular, one and a half stories and made of brick, with plank flooring and a steeply pitched roof. The jail and pillory (a wooden structure with cutouts for hands and heads that was used for public punishment) were to be placed near the spring, adjacent to the field known as Cold Water Run. (The ducking stool of the county, another device purposed to punish by social humiliation, was placed at Bermuda Hundred because Cold Water Run was too shallow to immerse lawbreakers.) Sadly, the original court building was torn down in 1917 but was replicated in 1977 as the county museum. The courthouse one sees facing Iron Bridge Road today is known as the 1917 courthouse, and the road it faces was originally known as Hundred Road.

East of the museum stand the 1828 and 1889 clerk's offices. The earlier two-room building had housed the county clerk for seventy years and later served as offices for the county treasurer, school board and commissioner of revenue. The 1889 building featured two fireproof vaults to protect the county records. These two buildings were joined in 1930 and now compose the county's Extension Office.

Also in 1930, the current Parks and Recreation building was erected to serve as the treasurer's office. At the southwest corner of the Green is the site of the original jail, built in 1783. Today this area is marked by brick pavers. The 1892 jail was one of a succession of jails and used some of the stone from an earlier building. It last held prisoners in 1962. The Chesterfield Historical Society of Virginia began meeting in the jail in the mid-1980s, but following lead paint abatement treatment and successive water issues in the 2000s, the jail was closed for several years. The year 2011 promises the reopening of the ground floor of the jail as an exhibit area for Police and Sheriff's Departments artifacts.

Chesterfield and the Revolution

It wasn't long after the county's formation before wartime shattered the tranquility of rural Chesterfield County. In December 1774, Chesterfield's involvement in war preparations began with sending 120 bushels of wheat to Boston. Soon after, in March 1775, Chesterfield citizens Archibald Cary and John Watkins were named delegates to the Richmond Convention, the second of five political meetings held throughout the state as a result of British governor Dunmore's dissolving of the House of Burgesses. Cary was named colonel of the Chesterfield battalion, which was headquartered on the grounds of the courthouse. This initiated the important role Chesterfield played in the Revolutionary War.

In 1780, there were six hundred men headquartered in the Chesterfield Camp, and Baron Frederick von Steuben assumed command. Von Steuben had been an inspector general and major general in the Continental army. A renowned expert in military drill and discipline who later wrote the *Revolutionary War Drill Manual*, Von Steuben had served as General Washington's chief of staff. Von Steuben had not been a general in his native Prussia; he had served in the extremely disciplined Prussian general headquarters as an aide-de-camp to the king. Finding himself unemployed after the Seven Years' War between Prussia and Great Britain, he became a chamberlain to Fürst Josef Friedrich Wilhelm of Hohenzollern-Hechingen, a county in southwestern Germany, where his career ended in scandal with charges of improper behavior with young boys.

Departing Germany for Paris, he met Benjamin Franklin, who sent him to America along with a letter of introduction to General Washington. Von Steuben went to Boston, where he volunteered to serve in the Continental cause without pay. He developed an innovative training model in which a small force would be trained and then sent to train others. A colorful character, he was known for his flamboyance and German cursing, which he had his aide translate into English so that his troops would know they were being chastised. He established organized and orderly camps, with latrines a safe distance away from tents and better sanitation—methods that remained in use for generations. His most important contribution to the Revolution was training the men in the use of the bayonet, a method that won more than one battle for the Americans. He came to Virginia in 1780 since the supplies and men were doled out from here.

The year 1781 found two hundred men in camp at Chesterfield Courthouse. In April, Major General William Phillips brought thirty-two ships and two thousand men to Portsmouth, from which they marched to Chesterfield Courthouse, burning the barracks, courthouse, jail, three hundred barrels of flour and several local houses. Although the courthouse was gutted, the county records were saved by the foresight of clerk Thomas Watkins. Phillips continued attacking and burning Chesterfield, defeating the Virginia navy, burning Osbornes Landing, Port Walthall and Manchester and moving toward Petersburg. Although by April 1781 General Lafayette had routed the terrorizing British troops from the outskirts of Richmond, the damage had been done at Chesterfield Courthouse, where little remained of the once vital supply station.

The Courthouses

The court resumed its business in 1780 at John Howlett's ordinary and decided to rebuild the courthouse, using the walls that still stood, with the addition of a large wing in the rear. The rebuilding was completed in 1783. The courthouse continued actively from 1783 until the Civil War. In 1864, Union forces under General August V. Kautz marched through the county, but they inflicted little damage, and the records of the court were once again saved due to the diligence of Nathan Cogbill, clerk of the court.

The county seat was moved to Manchester in 1871. When Manchester was incorporated in 1874, referendums that year and again in 1876 returned the county seat to its former location. The old courthouse had been renovated in the meantime, but before long it proved to be too small to contain the business of the growing county, and a new courthouse was approved by the board of supervisors and was erected in 1917. Although there was a contingent of citizens that lobbied for the preservation of the old building, those citizens did not prevail, and the old building was razed.

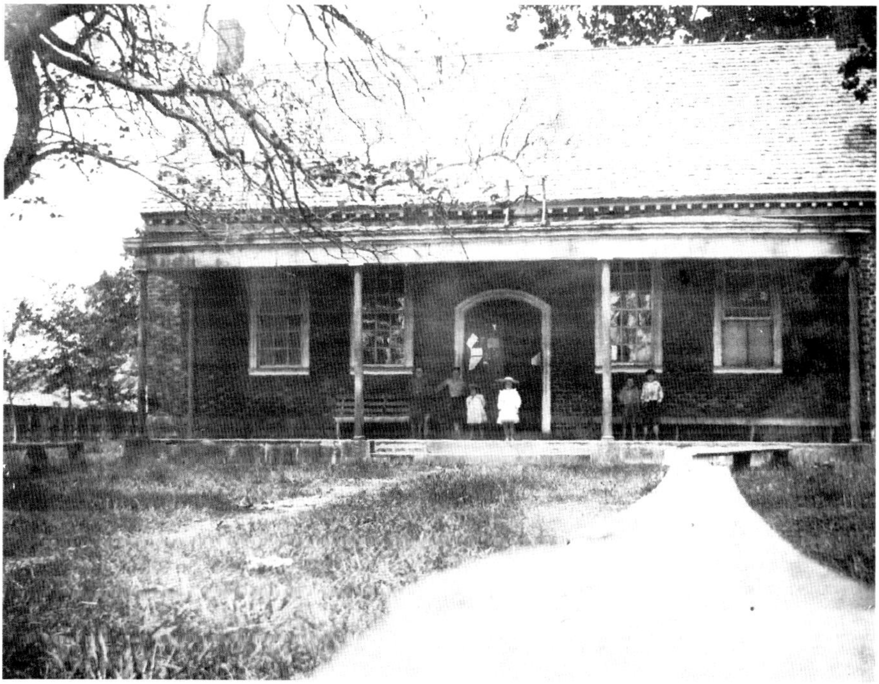

The 1750 courthouse. Taken before 1917, this photo shows children on the porch of the courthouse during court or market days. *Chesterfield Historical Society of Virginia.*

Twelve bids were placed in response to the ad for interested builders of the new courthouse in the Richmond and Petersburg newspapers, ranging from $15,498 to $21,842. The cornerstone was laid on October 26, 1917, during the annual county fair. The ceremony included an all-day picnic on the grounds, with a review of recently-drafted army recruits and speeches. This lovely and stately brick courthouse also was born during a period of war and again was used as a rallying point, or transfer station, of newly recruited soldiers in World War I. Completed in 1918, the brick rectangle measures eighty-five feet by forty-eight feet. It has a full basement and is topped by the cupola that peeks through the tall trees surrounding it today. The Chesterfield Historical Society used the building from 1990 until 2000. Serving in recent years as an overflow space for Chesterfield's juvenile court, structural weakness mandated its closure in 2008.

The building we know as Police Headquarters is actually the "new" courthouse of the 1950s. Bids on the project, planned to be a combination court and administrative office building, were taken in 1956. Included in the planned offices were those for the circuit court clerk, a police lockup and the sheriff's department. The 1917 courthouse was to be an administration building. The proposed cost was $340,000. Ten years later, in 1967, further growth required the building of an addition to the 1957 building to house the circuit court, county court, juvenile court and traffic court, along with a clerk's office. These were added to the back side of the courts building. The five-story administrative building was added in the late 1970s.

Monuments

Standing tall and proud above the Green is the Confederate Soldiers' Monument, built in 1903 by county Civil War veterans and supporters. Inscriptions read "Valor" and "Truthfulness," as well as "[I]t is sweet and honorable to die for one's country." According to an article in the *Times-Dispatch* on Sunday, August 30, 1903, three days before the unveiling ceremony,

> *some idea of the number of county people alone who have been long planning to witness the unveiling was gotten on last court day, when a proposition to unveil the monument on that day was discussed. Probably three hundred people were here at that time from all parts of the county, and at the suggestion of "taking the soldier's jacket off" at that time, there was a general howl of disapproval, those present contending that the people*

present then were not a handful compared with the crowd that had been eagerly looking forward to being present at the unveiling.

Indeed, the planning went all out for that midday event, with picnic tables scattered around the courtyard and a common sharing of potluck dishes "as long as the food lasts."

Following the usual speeches and prayers, the statue was unveiled. The statue had been in the planning since July 7, 1902, when a meeting of Confederate veteran county residents and friends of the Lost Cause was held to discuss the possibility of the statue. Prominent county residents and veterans J.M. Gregory, W.W. Baker, P.V. Cogbill, Dr. John B. Fisher and others headed the task force charged with raising public support and funding for the statue. Reported the *Times-Dispatch*: "[A]s is usual in such cases, the assistance of the ladies of the county was found to be

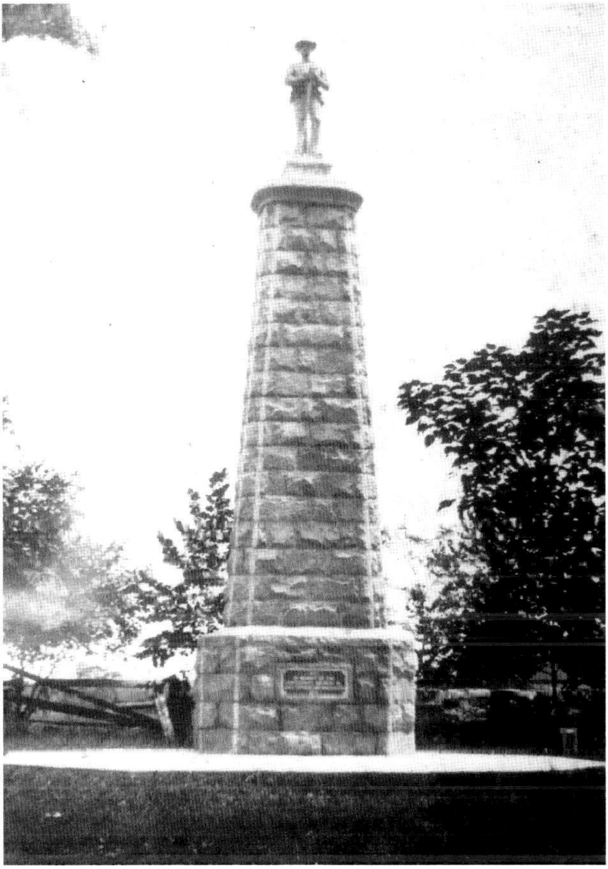

The Confederate Soldiers' Monument, September 3, 1903. This monument was erected by county Civil War veterans and supporters. *Chesterfield Historical Society of Virginia.*

indispensable in order to carry to a successful completion the work which lay so near to the hearts of those who were laboring for it." Once they were included in the planning of the monument, the paper reported, "then the work began to take on a lively aspect indeed." Originally planning to use granite from the walls of the old jail, the contractor was not pleased with those stones and used the freshly quarried stone from the quarries at Granite on the visible portion. The soldier on the top of the monument is made of zinc or white bronze, and he stands at parade rest. The base of the monument is surrounded by an octagonal concrete and mortar apron and "has been much admired by some competent critics."

Monument to the Baptist Preachers

In the mid-eighteenth century, most people were Anglican, but there were beginning to be ripples of dissent regarding the status quo, particularly in isolated areas that were located far from an established church but whose residents were still required to pay taxes for the support of their parish. The Toleration Act allowed laymen to apply for a license to preach, but some Separatist Baptists began to do so without following the law. In 1770, a group of vestrymen, who were the "watchdogs" of conformity to local laws, began persecuting itinerant preachers who did not apply for a license. Archibald Cary was a leader in this movement, and his name was found on most of the warrants issued against the offenders. Two young men, William Webber and Joseph Anthony from Goochland, were the first arrested. Given the opportunity to put up bond and be on "good behavior" for a year, they refused and chose to remain in jail for three months. Word of the men's imprisonment traveled throughout the area, and the two jailed men preached through the windows of the jail twice a week to large groups assembled outside, attracting both attention and converts. Today's Webber Memorial Baptist Church on Salem Church Road bears the name of the young dissident William.

The following year, Augustine Eastin was tried for preaching without a license, followed by John Tanner and John Weatherford in 1773. Patrick Henry is believed to have been responsible for the release of Weatherford. Jeremiah Walker was imprisoned in August 1773, and the last of the Baptists, David Tinsley, spent four months and sixteen days in jail in 1774. In the meantime, Colonel Cary had a high wall erected around the jail to keep curious congregants away. Whether made of wood or bricks and whether drums were actually beaten during the window-preaching is uncertain, but what remains is the record of a number of men who suffered persecution for the cause of freedom of religion in Chesterfield County—as well as a monument on the Courthouse Green to commemorate them. The monument to religious liberty was erected in 1925 by the Baptist community to honor the "apostles of religious liberty."

In 2005, a memorial stone was raised to honor Chesterfield police officers who died in the line of duty, as well as those who serve. This monolith was jointly funded by private and public resources.

The veterans' memorial wall is a twenty-first-century addition to the Courthouse Green. W. Baxter Perkinson Sr., a World War II veteran, was the visionary and driving force behind the wall. The first phase of construction was completed in 2000, and the wall was dedicated at the Veterans Day ceremony that November. The wall was a community-wide effort, with Perkinson's focused dedication to soliciting donations, along with the Chesterfield Historical Society of Virginia. Perkinson's son, Dr. Ivan Perkinson, painted a watercolor entitled *Remembering Veterans* to sell in the fundraising efforts, and partners from the board of supervisors, a local engineering and design firm and other local businesses and everyday citizens joined in the drive. Strategically placed benches dedicated to people who played integral roles in the construction of the wall, as well as to the wars in which America has fought, add interest and places for contemplation. The wall is featured in the yearly Veterans Day ceremony, where the names of soldiers lost in current military actions are permanently mounted in a place of honor.

Living Monument

Towering over the other greenery in the courthouse complex is the Nunnally oak tree. This white oak was planted in 1814 by county clerk Lawson Nunnally, who clerked for the county from 1812 to 1820. Beginning in 1916, the tree was measured and the dimensions were entered into the court record. Ground rules for this event dictate that the tree is measured 5 feet above the ground. In 1981, the circumference was 16 feet, 4.5 inches and in 2001 it was 17 feet, 3 inches. Cared for by arborists and fondly looked after by occupants of the nearby Extension Office, the tree is due for measuring in 2011.

Although located at the bustling center of Chesterfield's commerce and government life, all county citizens should make it a point to visit this tranquil and historic square. As the insightful wanderer follows the old, uneven brick paths, stepping over tree roots and maybe catching sight of the resident cat, G.W., it only takes a little imagination to hear the whispers of soldiers, the pounding of a wooden gavel, the scratch of a quill on parchment or the sighs of prisoners long released. Come visit Chesterfield, and start right here at its heart.

Prominent People and Popular Places: How Chesterfield Schools Got Their Names

The students of Chesterfield history with just a little creative curiosity drive through neighborhoods and down streets with names whose origins they ponder, past businesses that tell the story of local commerce and by schools that memorialize people they don't know. The curious citizen can do a little detective work at his local library or historical society and can learn a lot about Chesterfield's past from the names he finds on our county schools.

Many local schools bear the names of the communities they serve, such as Bensley Elementary, named after the village founded in 1888 by developers A.W. and R.C. Bensley, who built Chesterfield's first planned community. Bon Air, French for "good air," was a popular Victorian resort town in the late 1800s. Clover Hill High School takes its name from the home in the Winterpock community that was built about 1775 and renamed for its rampant growth of clover by owner Mrs. Martha Reid Cox about 1834. The village of Midlothian got its name from an area in southern Scotland, which also has East Lothian and West Lothian settlements. Sir Walter Scott was a famous resident of Mid Lothian, Scotland.

Naming schools after prominent citizens is a common practice, and some of Chesterfield's thus honored citizens have interesting stories. Andrew Martin Davis took some time to track down, but members of his church, Providence Methodist, can tell you about this popular man whose likeness is on a stained-glass window in their building. A farmer and the owner of much of the land east of Providence Road (originally called Church Road) between Routes 60 and 360, he was called "Grandpa Davis" by the children who knew that he always had candy in his pockets to share. Early settler James Bailey arrived in Chesterfield before 1736, when it was still part of Henrico. The census map of 1880 shows the Bailey name in several places, from the Skinquarter area to where present-day Bailey Bridge school is located. The bridge, long gone, was presumably over Swift Creek.

Supervisor of Elementary Education Marguerite Christian brought Project Head Start to Chesterfield County in 1966. The program,

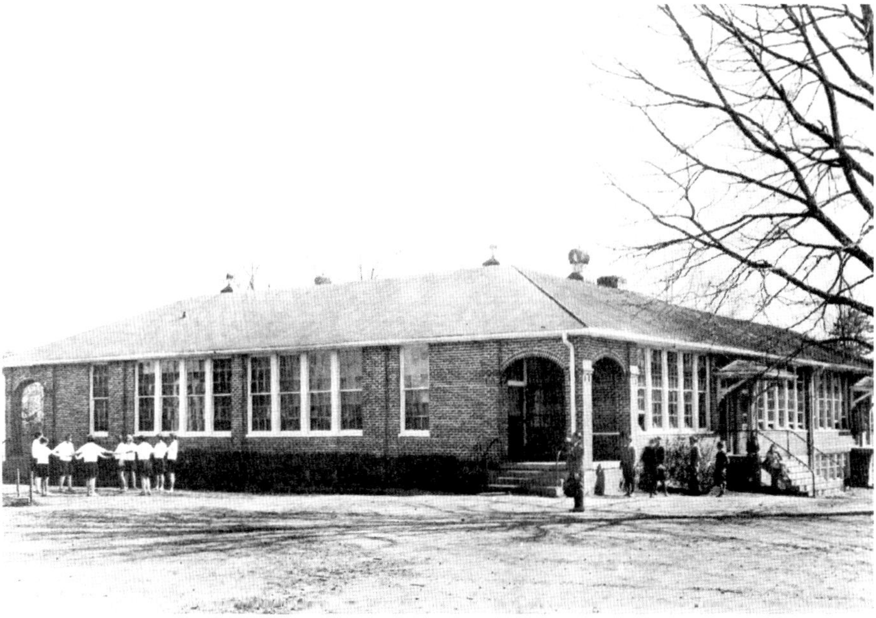

Midlothian High School, circa 1929. This brick structure was built circa 1920 as Chesterfield's second high school and replaced a frame structure built circa 1910. *Chesterfield Historical Society of Virginia.*

serving preschool children from low-income families, had been used and discontinued at a school in Midlothian. A group of teachers, ministers and parents met with a Washington, D.C., representative of the Head Start program who encouraged them to apply for a grant. The deadline for the application was the following Monday. Working all weekend, this group prepared the application, typed by Mrs. Christian and hand-postmarked by the post office late Sunday evening. The result was a $20,000 grant that enabled the program to be restarted in a local church. When the new superintendent of schools visited the program in its church home, he ordered that it be moved back across the street to its original school in Midlothian. Christian, ever the determined champion of underprivileged children, was honored with an elementary school in her name in the southern part of Chesterfield.

Another former educator and historian shares her name with a Chesterfield elementary school. Bettie Woodson Weaver has written several books focused on local history and natural resources in central Virginia, including a local history textbook. Her recently published *The Continental Training Depot and General Rendezvous at Chesterfield Courthouse, Virginia (1780–1781) with rosters of*

Chesterfield County Revolutionary War Officers and Troops from 1775 to 1783 is the latest contribution Mrs. Weaver has made to the chronicling of local history.

Chesterfield's Native American heritage is honored by schools named for the Monacan tribe who inhabited northern Chesterfield before the arrival of the English settlers. Local historical figure Pocahontas is honored with two schools named for her—both middle and high schools in the southern end of the county bear her Indian name, "Matoaca."

While Thomas Dale and L.C. Bird represent well-known and respected leaders in Chesterfield—Dale as the marshal of Virginia in 1611 who established Bermuda Hundred and Henricus and Bird who served as a twentieth-century Virginia state senator—two local schools are named after a figure from one of Chesterfield's biggest scandals: Anthony Robiou was murdered by his father-in-law in 1851 for his alleged abuse of his young wife.

African Americans have always valued education, some risking their lives by learning and teaching reading and writing. Chesterfield's schools were segregated until 1970, with one high school for black students, named after George Washington Carver. This school was a merger of D. Webster Davis and Hickory Hill Highs. Now named Chesterfield Community High, the Carver name is still used for the middle school in Chester.

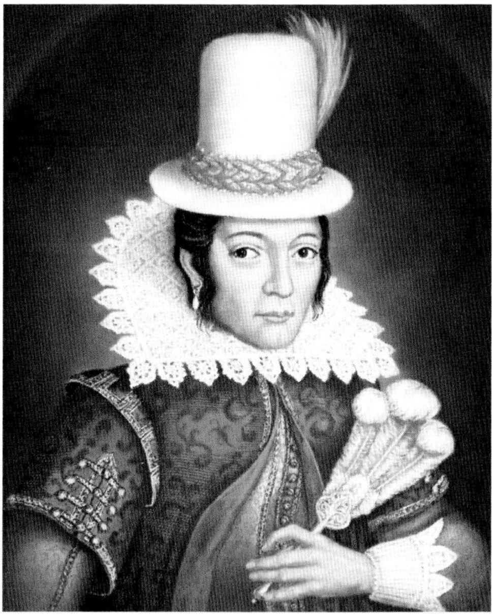

Indian princess Pocahontas. Photograph of a painting by William Sheppard, copyright Detroit Publishing Company. *Library of Congress.*

The C.E. Curtis Elementary School was named for a former chairman of the Chesterfield County School Board. It was built in 1959 and represents an interesting era in the county's school system. The late 1950s brought a population boom to Chesterfield, with an expanding school-age population. The school board was faced with the dilemma of how to serve these children. About 1,300 new students entered school in September 1956 in Chesterfield. There wasn't enough space in existing school buildings to hold all of the students, and rooms in churches, community centers and private clubs were rented. Some children attending (in name only) a particular school couldn't even tell you the school's name, as they had never actually entered the building, and many were inside the official school building only for homeroom period before being bused elsewhere. In response to this urgent situation, the board voted in 1957 to build five new schools and to make additions to eleven others.

In the meantime, the Supreme Court was hearing *Brown v. the Board of Education*, and Chesterfield's school board, along with its legislators, was watching to see how the desegregation mandate would affect the county and whether money raised in bond issues would be made available to all schools or just those not integrated. Several groups proposed solutions to the overcrowding situation, and the school bond issue of 1956 became the first bond issue to be voted down by county voters. Construction was on hold, teachers were unsure of their status and citizens pondered how to get their children educated. Schools went to second shifts, and the board faced a shortage of 127 classrooms. Four years after the previous bond issue, bids put out for school construction were coming in much higher than the amount the bonds had raised. The school board asked the board of supervisors for deficit financing; the board of supervisors turned it down. Finally, the citizens of Chesterfield took matters into their own hands and formed a coalition called Better Schools for Chesterfield. Its platform was a new bond referendum. The school board and the board of supervisors endorsed it, and $4,500,000 was approved. Curtis, Hening, Southampton and Harrowgate Elementaries were opened in 1959.

As most history detectives know, there's always more to the story. Chesterfield had four types of schools in the colonial period. The private plantation school, the community school, the free school and the apprenticeship system all gave residents several educational options. Many tiny rural schoolhouses were in use until the twentieth century, and several still stand today. Now home to a community college, private and public schools, alternate-learning environments, home schools and other educational enterprises, our exemplary county school system is truly a reflection of the richness of our county's history.

Part II
PEOPLE

CHESTERFIELD NATIVE SON: JOHN RANDOLPH

Fiery orator and natural leader John Randolph was known for his outrageous comments, most famous of which was, "I am an aristocrat. I love liberty, I hate equality." Born in what is now Hopewell in 1773 as the son of a wealthy tobacco planter of the same name, young John's birthplace was called Cawsons, and it was the home of Randolph's mother, Frances Bland. The Randolph family home in Chesterfield was called Matoax after a Randolph ancestor, Pocahontas.

John Randolph's father, John Sr., was from "Curles" on the James. John Sr. died when his son was just a child, and he grew very close to his mother. He said of her, "She was the only person who ever understood me." And he was a difficult man to understand. Possibly due to an affliction of some sort during childhood, Randolph never reached physical maturity; he was beardless and had a high-pitched voice. It has been theorized that he may have had Klinefelters syndrome, in which a male child has an extra X chromosome that sometimes manifests in a spectrum of physical and behavioral symptoms.

Randolph was educated by private tutors, followed by study at the College of New Jersey and Columbia College and then law school in Philadelphia. He never practiced the law but was elected to the sixth Congress at the young age of twenty-six. Randolph was portrayed by his Congressional contemporaries as a small man, resembling his famous ancestor Pocahontas, and was ridiculed by his enemies but was a formidable opponent. It appears that Mr. Randolph was not a jolly, pleasant man and that he had fallouts with men like Thomas Jefferson over the political issue of federalism versus nationalism or republicanism. Once allied with Jefferson, they became bitter enemies as Jefferson believed in a strong government and Randolph in a society guided by the elite. Randolph's confrontational manner was a barrier to his effectiveness.

Despite being a natural leader and orator, Randolph was considered an outsider and an eccentric by his contemporaries. He drank heavily, used opium and was constantly in poor health until he died from tuberculosis in 1833. He was a flashy dresser and often brought an entourage of slaves and hunting dogs to Congress. He once fought a duel with Henry Clay, of whom he said, "[T]his being, so brilliant yet so corrupt, which, like a rotten mackerel by moonlight, shined and stunk." Randolph was not well liked, and his small, immature physical stature was hardly a come-on to women, and yet he was a poet and a lover with a singing voice that some called the loveliest ever heard.

In a little-known Chesterfield love story, Randolph seemed to have loved and lost in his youth. When he was about eight years old, Virginia was invaded by Benedict Arnold, and reports of his atrocities were rife. Randolph's mother fled with her family to Winterpock, to the home of Benjamin Ward Jr., and it was here where John met Maria Ward. Before fire destroyed Winterpock, they were said to have played together blissfully ignorant of the crisis surrounding them. As not-too-far distant neighbors, one can imagine that John and Maria saw each other frequently in subsequent years. They worshiped together, and their mothers were friends. It's no wonder that the mothers probably encouraged the romance between their children.

As cruel fate would have it, John renounced his love of Maria, presumably because he knew that his physical defect made a normal life impossible for them. Upon taking his leave of Maria, he slashed his horse's reins from their tie with his knife and rode wildly and angrily away. Maria's father, not understanding the cause for his daughter's jilting, challenged Randolph for a duel, until Randolph candidly told him the truth. Maria, called the greatest belle of her day in Virginia, married another Randolph, Peyton, son of General Washington's secretary of state. She had children and still has descendants around this part of Virginia. She was also supposedly wooed by General Lafayette when he visited Richmond. Maria died young and had given John Randolph's love letters to a mutual friend with the instructions to burn them upon

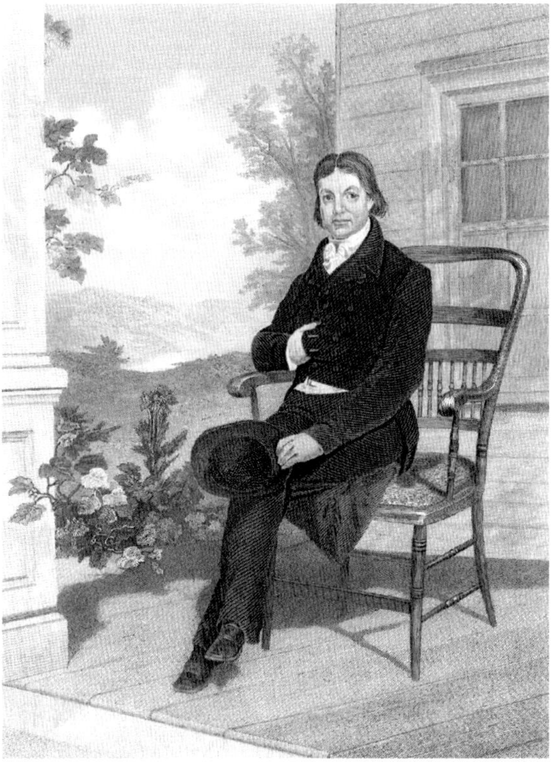

John Randolph. From the original painting by Chappel in the possession of Johnson, Fry & Company, Publishers, New York, circa 1863. *Library of Congress.*

her death without breaking the seal with which they were bound. The letters were as genial and the words as soft as Randolph's Congressional rantings were harsh and aggressive. Until his death many years after Maria's, Randolph called her his angel and lamented in a letter read by friends after his death: "I loved, aye, and was loved again not wisely, but too well."

CHESTERFIELD'S OTHER SETTLERS: THE HUGUENOTS

Many of Chesterfield's native sons, those whose families' names are borne on street signs, subdivisions and schools, figure that their ancestors came from England. Every schoolchild knows that this is the country from which the original colonists came in the early 1600s. Many may not know that there were early settlers from other countries, as well, and that they may, in fact, have French blood running through their veins.

Religious Refugees

Like the English, many French refugees came to this New World seeking freedom to worship God in their chosen manner. The state of traditional religion in Europe had changed in 1517 when Martin Luther published his *Ninety-Five Theses*, the work in which he criticized the Catholic Church. The changes that this document sparked led to religious wars for the next 131 years. The Holy Roman Empire, the area we know now as Germany, Switzerland, Belgium, Czechoslovakia, the Netherlands, Austria and parts of other modern-day countries, was the hardest hit by the holy wars. The Reformation movement led by Luther swept through the Holy Roman Empire and soon into France.

France was a theocracy, a system in which religious leaders were looked at as having divine authority in ruling the country, and the king was a staunch Catholic. Members of the middle and upper classes soon embraced Protestantism, with its promise of individual faith and salvation that was not dependent on the rule of the church, and this led to vast accusations of heresy and calls for the extermination of dissenters to the Catholic Church.

These "heretics," known as Huguenots in France, continued to grow in number and influence until 1562, when 1,200 of them were killed at Vassey. War ravaged France for the next thirty-five years. Finally, the Edict of Nantes designated certain areas of France in which Protestantism was allowed, and relative peace reigned for the next eighty or so years. The infamous Louis XIV revoked the edict in 1685, and the persecution began again, leading to mass exodus of Frenchmen into Germany, the Netherlands, England and even South Africa.

While refugees in these countries were considered "temporary" guests who were waiting for France to relax its persecution, many were vigorously recruited to go to the New World. Virginia, especially, was anxious for more settlers and even offered additional land to those who went back to England to recruit. President John Jay of the Huguenot Society of America wrote in 1885 that King Louis lost "by means similarly atrocious, hundreds of thousands of those same heretics, who carried industry, intelligence and prosperity, light, truth and happiness to other lands, including our own." Many of these refugees who ended up in America settled in New York, Pennsylvania, Virginia and North Carolina. They came in groups or individually. Some came from French settlements in other countries, some from the French West Indies and others from other American colonies. These people were craftsmen and artisans, as well as professional people, and they were welcomed into the areas in which they settled. Of the refugees who settled in what is now Chesterfield at the turn of the eighteenth century, many had initially fled France for England and had supported William of Orange in that country, in return for which William (King William III) granted them lands in the New World.

Arrivals in 1700

Several shiploads of immigrants settled just west of Richmond, at the site of the old Monacan Indian settlement in a town they named Manakintowne. This was an area that the English were happy to see settled with white-skinned immigrants, as the nearness of Indians threatened growth to the west. The Monacans continued to reside in the vicinity until about 1722. Bringing in this entirely new group of settlers provided a nice buffer by a community that was markedly different from the British settlers yet had

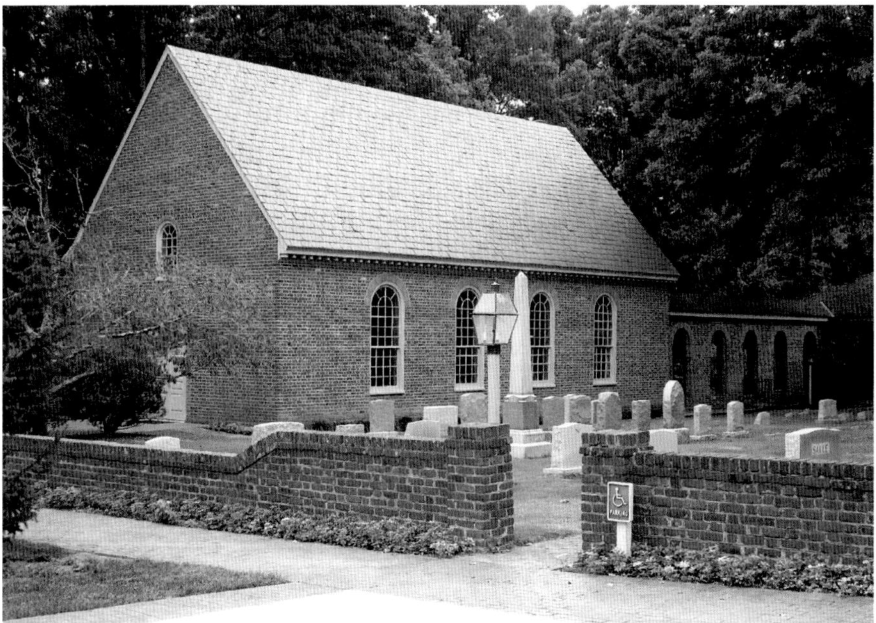

Manakin Episcopal Church, built in 1954. *Peter Lipowicz.*

been assimilated into the English culture and the Church of England by virtue of their years in exile from France. The village of ten thousand acres, whose land patents were issued between 1711 and 1757 by William Byrd II of Tuckahoe, was divided into farms that ran lengthwise down to the James River, with one of the choicest lots being set aside for the minister. The church, designed by a Swiss traveler, was built in the center of the settlement, and here they worshiped twice a day on Sundays. They called their parish King William. Several churches followed, and the present church, Manakin Episcopal, was built in 1954 in the style of William Byrd's chapel at Westover. On its lovely grounds still stands the library of the Huguenot Society of the Founders of Manakin in the Colony of Virginia, as well as the 1895 chapel.

Early Artisans

The Huguenot settlers provided their new country with silk work, weaving and lace making and other professional trades, as well as noblemen. In 1702, they began a wine made of the wild grapes in the area's woods, producing a claret "of good flavor." The early years of the settlement were lean. At one point, corn sent by William Byrd kept the settlers from starvation, but they soon learned how to clear land, plant and harvest.

Although they were not farmers, they adapted to the land and culture easily and became well assimilated, leaving very few traces of their native land or culture for us to see today. Of the nearly eight hundred French Huguenots who settled in Chesterfield, each family received 133 acres and was excused from paying taxes for seven years, in order to encourage them to put down roots. Interestingly, the availability of a subsidy of meal that could be obtained at the Bermuda Hundred seaport brought the Huguenots through the county on Indian trails that later were worn down into roadways—the most well known of which is Buckingham Road, now known as Midlothian Turnpike. Others followed Falling Creek as it wound its way from the James to Manakintowne. In this way, the Huguenots soon migrated throughout the county, which perhaps aided in their easy assimilation. The fact that the settlement existed as a Huguenot enclave for such a brief period of time is a testimony to the easy integration of the refugees, as well as to the value with which their skills were regarded in encouraging their migration throughout Chesterfield County.

Chesterfield Huguenots

Although many of the names have become anglicized over time or were misspelled originally as a result of phonetic interpretation, some names of early Huguenot settlers are interwoven throughout Chesterfield's history. Flournoy, Jouett, Lacy, Perdue, Michie, Salle, LaPrade, Young, DuVal, Crostic, Morrissett and Martin are a few. Antoine Trabue was a coal mine operator who opened a tavern on the main thoroughfare of Buckingham Road. This facility housed stagecoach travelers, as well as people involved in the coal mines, and has undergone major restoration work by a Trabue descendant today. Antoine's grandson, Daniel, kept a journal in which he recorded his family's stories.

The earliest discovery of coal in Chesterfield is reported to have been as early as 1701, when a Huguenot settler kicked loose some dirt on the riverside and found a ledge of bituminous coal. This area formed the northern edge of the coal area in Midlothian. Aetna Hill, built in 1791 by Thompson Blunt and his wife, Huguenot descendant Frances Morrisette,

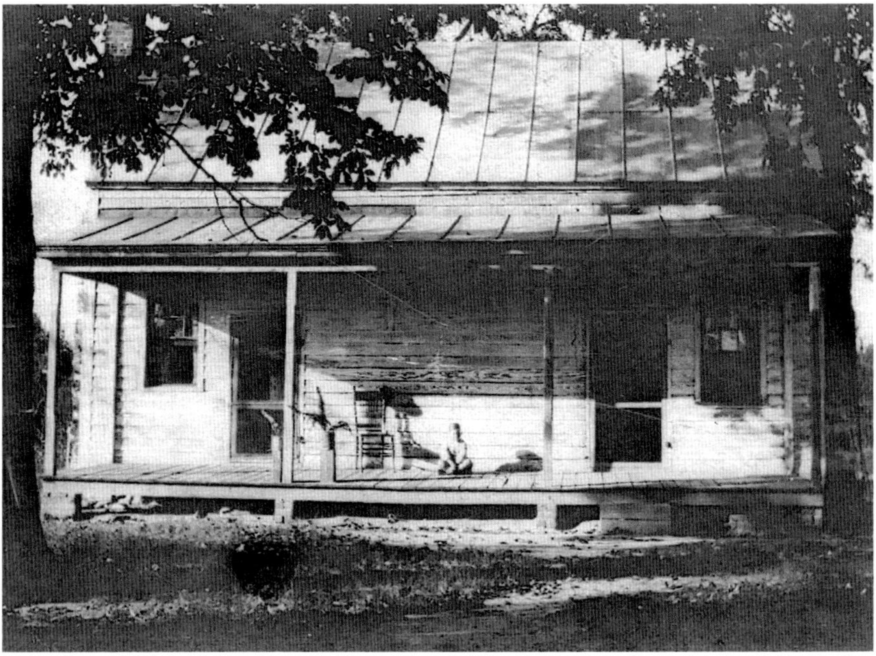

Huguenot house with two front doors, probably built by Francis Flournoy in the eighteenth century. The land is currently covered by Route 288. *Chesterfield Historical Society of Virginia.*

was named for Blunt's Aetna coal mines. Matthew Jouett was a fourth-generation portrait painter. Land patent books from the county of Henrico (of which Chesterfield was a part until 1749) show 574 acres of land being patented in 1705 to Abraham Michaux; 232 acres to Abraham Salle; and 17,650 acres on Falling Creek to John Tullit—who was also a miner of coal. At the time, this last patent was the largest ever offered. William Moseley, for whom the present-day community is named, patented 760 acres on Skinquarter Creek in the early 1700s.

The Huguenot settlers brought a new style of architecture with them to this country. Their houses were frame with end chimneys, dormer windows and sloping roofs. Some of the Huguenot houses had two front side-by-side doors. Houses that show the Huguenot influence can still be seen in the northwestern part of our county today, and many of our Chesterfield friends and neighbors, some unwittingly, bear the names of these brave, refined and flexible settlers from another part of the Old World.

Chesterfield Families in the Civil War: Sesquicentennial Stories

A century and a half after it began, the Civil War still has a large presence in Chesterfield County—and don't look for things to change in the next few years. The Virginia General Assembly created the Virginia Sesquicentennial of the American Civil War Commission in 2006 to prepare for and commemorate the sesquicentennial of Virginia's participation in the American Civil War, as well as the end of slavery and emancipation. Our county boasts the only locality in the nation within whose boundaries an entire campaign was fought, and our several Civil War sites will be popular spots for visitors and residents alike to learn about the war. Perhaps they will also learn some of the stories of families who gave beyond measure for the cause of states' rights.

When coal was discovered in the Winterpock area of Chesterfield in 1837, land immediately became very valuable, and the little community of Winterpock grew into a boomtown of nearly one thousand residents. Within that community was a family named Patram. Elizabeth Patram was young enough to require her father's consent when she wed Daniel Patram in 1817. She gave birth to two daughters, Minnie and Martha, followed by sons Edward (1827), Richard (1832) and Robert (1840), as well as another daughter, Susan, in between. They lived in the Summit area of Winterpock.

Summit was a railroad station on Beach Road, and there is a present-day road with that name near Clover Hill plantation.

We know that the Patrams had at least three sons who fought together in the bloody war, and census documents indicate that there may have been more. Although censuses in the early 1800s do not list family members by name, over the course of thirty years, six male children were counted on one or more of the surveys. Edward, Richard and Robert can be accounted for through pension applications many years after the war. Edward served in the Fourteenth Virginia Regiment of Infantry and was wounded in the Battle of Malvern Hill (where he was shot through the back), at Gettysburg (where he was shot in the head), at Drewry's Bluff and, finally, at Five Forks (both of which resulted in chest wounds). His pension application reports, "I am disabled from any manual labor from weakness in the chest and shortness of breath" but that, at age sixty-one, "I can ably do a little work."

Caroline Patram, widow of Robert, who served in the "company commanded by Captain James Snead" (Company I, Fourteenth Virginia Infantry), filed for her widow's pension in 1900. Married to her veteran husband in 1882, she was left widowed in 1899 when he died of "paralysis," and she applied for his pension of twenty-five dollars annually. Richard Patram served in the Forty-first Virginia Regiment and was wounded on December 13, 1862, at the Battle of Fredericksburg, where his left arm was removed "at the sholder [*sic*] joint." Richard's pension of thirty dollars was awarded in 1888, when he was fifty-six years old.

Scott Williams, the Chesterfield Historical Society of Virginia's Military History committee chairman, reported on the planning of the sesquicentennial in Chesterfield County. A committee has been formed consisting of representatives from county government, the Chesterfield Historical Society of Virginia, Chesterfield Heritage Alliance, the National Park Service, the Richmond Metropolitan Convention and Visitors Bureau and Petersburg Area Regional Tourism. The goal of the committee is to highlight both the military campaigns and the effects of the war on the homefront. "By telling the stories of soldiers and civilians, we hope to reach a broader, more diverse audience," Williams reported. The committee is also working on developing special exhibits for local libraries that will tell the story of the soldiers who fought and the civilians who endured the hardships brought on by the war. In addition, the committee is working with the Chesterfield Central Library on scanning historic documents pertaining to the Civil War, as well as a commemorative vigil to remember those who lost their lives during the Civil War. An enthusiastic Williams said, "We hope to have a number of other events between now and 2015 as we mark the important role Chesterfield had during the war."

On the south side of Swift Creek, in central Chesterfield, is land that belonged to Joseph Bailey in 1862. Bailey erected a house on the property about the time of the Civil War in the area of today's Bailey Bridge Road. The Baileys were a large family with deep roots in Chesterfield's history and on whom a good deal of research has been done. They represent one of the many families who lent multiple sons to the Confederate cause.

According to the Bailey family history book, written and researched by Mary Ellen Howe, "The year 1861 brought the cruel reality of the Civil War to Chesterfield County. All able-bodied men in the Skinquarter area joined the Confederate forces." In May of that year, five of Josiah Bailey's sons were mustered into service. Thomas, Joseph, James, John and William were part of Mahone's Brigade. Muster records show Thomas Bailey as a carpenter after his enlistment in 1861, at age thirty, working on winter quarters. Thomas died on June 2, 1862, of wounds he received at the Battle of Seven Pines, leaving three sons and a daughter.

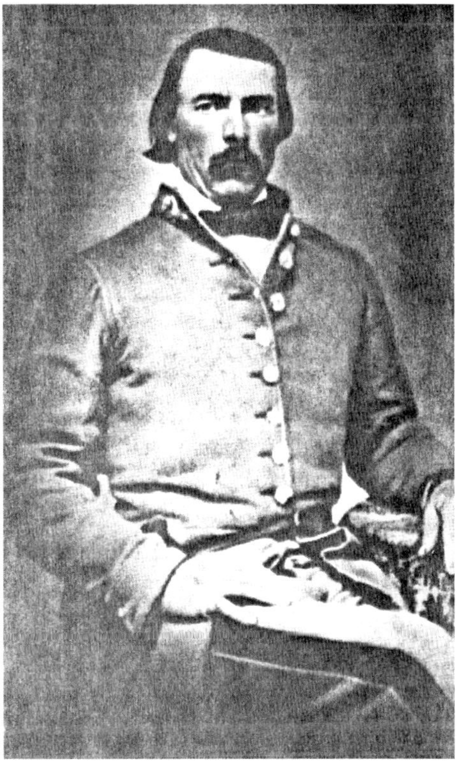

Thomas Edward Bailey in Confederate uniform. Born in 1829 on a Genito Road farm, Bailey served in the Sixth Virginia Regiment, Company K, was killed in battle and was buried at his birthplace. *Chesterfield Historical Society of Virginia.*

Ms. Howe wrote, "The four surviving Bailey brothers returned to Chesterfield County to continue their lives." James enlisted in May 1861, at about age twenty-one, for one year and reenlisted the following year. Wounded at Burgess Mill in 1864, he survived to become a lumberman and sawmill owner and owned several thousand acres of land in Chesterfield, which he left to his sons. After his first wife died, he married her sister and had five sons.

John Alexander went back to farming and also ran a sawmill. John had three sons and two daughters and is buried in the cemetery at Mount Hermon Baptist Church on Genito Road. Brother William was only eighteen when he enlisted with his brothers in 1861. William, who was detailed as a cook, was wounded at the Battle of the Crater. He became a farmer in Powhatan. The least prolific of the Bailey boys, he fathered twin daughters. Joseph, who enlisted in 1862 at about age twenty-six and "paid own travel expenses to muster, $4.40," was wounded at Malvern Hill, as well as at the Wilderness in 1864, and returned home to farming. Marrying in 1866, he also had five children. All five Bailey brothers served in the Sixth Virginia Infantry, part of Mahone's Brigade, one of Virginia's premier units.

Chesterfield residents know that the Civil War was fought in their backyard, but there is a human side to the story that makes this war more real to twenty-first-century students. Many people know that large houses were commonly used as hospitals—homes such as West View, Dellwood and Warfield. Dellwood and Clover Hill plantations served as refugee centers. The Yellow House in Chester had its doors taken down by Federal troops, who used them for stretchers. General Benjamin Butler had a Union military hospital built at Point of Rocks. Houses like the Halfway House were used at different times as temporary headquarters for one or the other of the forces. The lesser-known social side of the war is illustrated by the stalemate over the Howlett Line, where soldiers "traded goods, food, and anecdotes along with bullets," according to Jeffrey O'Dell's *Chesterfield County: Early Architecture and Historic Sites*. O'Dell also reported on a story from an early twentieth-century newspaper account:

> *Between the (Ware Bottom) church and (Parker's) battery, there was a very large, magnificent spring, at least six feet in diameter and two feet deep. This spring was sheltered in a valley between the two lines and was the trysting ground for both armies, for there was a code of ethics existing between the two armies at this place that either side could approach the spring if they came without arms, and there could be seen all day long the Blue and Gray assembling at this spring with large canteens to be filled with cool water and carried back to their respective lines. Often on these occasions they would tarry too long, and when the cause of the tarrying was ascertained it would be found that the boys in Blue and Gray were playing cards at the Spring; many a game of poker and seven-up decided the ownership of tobacco and coffee. Such familiarity existed between the two lines that it had to be broken up and only a few allowed to go from either line to secure the water.*

Clearly, the war was a tragedy in our young nation, and the toll it took on families on both sides can't be romanticized. General Lee's battered army entered Chesterfield in the Ettrick area on April 3, 1865, on the way to Appomattox. It traveled River Road to Winterpock before turning north toward Amelia County. Judge James Cox of Clover Hill plantation learned of the proximity of the general's troops and invited Lee and his staff to lunch, an occasion written about by Cox's daughter in her memoir, *My Confederate Girlhood.* Upon their departure the next day, "Mrs. P," presumably the mother of the Patram brothers, accosted the general to cry, "Oh, General Lee, what's become of my Dolly?" Kate Virginia Cox Logan's account continued, "[D]ivining at once that Dolly must be not a toy but a soldier, the general, forgetting for the moment his own overwhelming troubles, replied courteously and sympathetically: 'Madame, if you will tell me your Dolly's name and his company and command, I shall try to find him for you.'" Each poor Confederate woman considered that General Lee was the protector of her individual son.

Bands of brothers—families whose names are still heard in Chesterfield today, houses we drive by daily and battles with familiar names. All tell the sad story of the war fought right here in Chesterfield.

Famous Murders in Chesterfield County

The taking of one life by another is always a tragedy. There have been too many such crimes in the local spotlight in recent times, and it's easy to feel a wistful nostalgia for life in a simpler, more innocent time. That rosy picture doesn't stand up to the light of reality, however, as evidenced by these crimes of passion in earlier Chesterfield days.

Martha Morrisett

It was April 1806 when the inquisition of slaves Sarah and Cillae was held. (These names, recorded in court documents, are uncertain; Mrs. Morrisett had a slave named Creesy, but there is no record of one named Sarah. These women are also referred in court documents as Sall and Creese.) Widow Martha Morrisett had been missing for a while, and several neighboring men began a search for her. To their horror, they found blood on the ground near the edge of the James River where it bounded

Morrisett's property. Upon close examination, they also found pieces of flesh and bone. A group of searchers was assembled, and for quite a while, members dragged the river for a body, at last finding some random body parts. Two legs, one thigh, part of an arm and three other unidentifiable pieces were finally discovered.

Questioning of the slaves of the home began, to no avail, until the questioners found Cillae, who responded to their questions by exclaiming, "I could not help it, I was not in fault, I ought not to be blamed." She went on to explain that she and another slave were plowing when Morrisett approached and began to chastise (beat) her. After Morrisett had left, Cillae found Sarah and complained about her treatment, declaring that she intended to run away. Sarah advised her against it and recommended killing their mistress instead.

Returning to her plowing, Cillae was soon set upon again by Morrisett, to which she responded by physically pushing Morrisett away. Sarah advanced upon the struggling women and knocked her mistress down with an axe. She delivered several blows and covered her unresponsive body under some bushes. After nightfall, Cillae, Sarah and Jim, Sarah's husband, carried Morrisett's body to the river, where Sarah and Jim cut her up and threw the pieces in the water.

Under questioning, Sarah admitted that Morrisett had called to her for help during the squabble with Cillae but asserted that Cillae had been the one to "put her [Morrisett] away." Sarah's husband, Jim, called up by the women to help them dispose of the body, testified at his inquest that he had told the women that "if they had undertaken anything, they must go through with it, and asked Sarah no questions."

Chesterfield County Will Book 6, Inquisition of Murder, reported, "Sarah and Cillae, not having God before their eyes, but being moved and seduced by the instigation of the Devil, on Tuesday the first day of April in the Thirtieth year of the Commonwealth, with force and arms, being comforted, aided, and abetted by Jim…made and assault" upon Morrisett, which caused her immediate death.

Clerk of Court Thomas Watkins recorded that Sarah was tried, convicted and sentenced to be executed on the spot where the murder was committed on the second Friday in July; Cillae was tried, convicted and sentenced to be executed on the last Friday in May in Manchester. Jim was tried and acquitted.

Henry T. Miller

On the banks of Chesterfield's other river, the Appomattox, stands a brick house once owned by a murderer. The 750-acre plantation near Chesterfield's border with Amelia was built about 1826 and sold a dozen years later to Mr. Henry T. Miller. Miller had an overseer, James Mosely Stratton, who shot and killed Miller in the fall of 1856, possibly over an adulterous relationship with Stratton's wife. Court records do not confirm the motive, instead citing an argument between employer and employee over the picking of corn without permission. The fact that Stratton shot his employer twice, as well as that witnesses had seen Miller enter Stratton's house earlier that day in Stratton's absence, led to the commonly held belief that it was indeed a crime of retribution.

It took ten days to choose a jury in the Miller killing, and the trial lasted three weeks. Stratton was indicted for involuntary manslaughter and found guilty on October 31, 1856. His sentence was one day in jail.

Miller had been one of the wealthiest men in Chesterfield, with holdings of 1,114 acres and a personal estate valued at $26,908. He owned thirty-one slaves and many shares of stock in the Richmond and Petersburg Railroad. He learned, however, that he couldn't have everything he wanted.

John Hampden Pleasants

In 1846, Thomas Ritchie Jr. was acquitted of the murder of John Hampden Pleasants, editor of the *Whig* and the *New Compiler*. The party of Abraham Lincoln, Whigs took a stance against the practice and spread of slavery, among other ideologies. Slavery was a hotly disputed topic of the time, and the practice was both defended and attacked with fervor by many southerners. Ritchie was the editor of the influential *Richmond Enquirer*, one of the predecessors of the *Times-Dispatch*, which he had purchased in 1804. Ritchie ran the very successful newspaper for forty-one years and boasted a readership that included Thomas Jefferson.

Although not an abolitionist, Ritchie was in favor of the gradual emancipation of slaves. Pleasants's antislavery zeal demanded freedom at once. Ritchie's paper insinuated that Pleasants was going to start an abolitionist paper in Richmond; Pleasants denied this. A Washington correspondent known as "Macon" became a part of the feud, along with some columnists of Philadelphia newspapers, which were very interested in slavery issues. The men's ongoing disagreement was played out in their respective newspapers at length and ran an almost inevitable path to the dueling field. Their vicious argument erupted in an editorial by Ritchie stating that Pleasants was hiding behind his children in cowardice and comparing him to King Herod in his abolitionist fervor. Pleasants replied through the newspaper, letting Ritchie know that he would be waiting on the Chesterfield side of the James River at sunrise on February 25, armed and accompanied by two similarly armed friends. Purportedly, Pleasants was equipped with a sword cane, two dueling pistols, a revolver and a bowie knife, while Ritchie carried a Roman sword and several pistols. Ritchie ended up walking away unharmed, while Pleasants was felled by five bullets. Ritchie fled to Washington, only to return after Pleasants had died, two days later, to turn himself in. Filled with remorse, he left $25,000 to Pleasants's daughter upon his death two years later. Thus ended a contentious political enmity between members of the press, most of whom these days do battle with less lethal armaments.

Anthony Robiou

Possibly the best-known Chesterfield murder story involved love, lust and the role of women in antebellum society. Emily Wormeley was only fourteen when her father signed for her to marry his friend, Anthony Robiou, forty-five years old. The young bride and her much older husband lived together in less-than-newlywed harmony for two years in Bellgrade Plantation, now home to a Ruth's Chris steakhouse. Robiou claimed to have returned home unexpectedly one day to find his bride alone with nineteen-year-old John Reid. The Robious were reputed to have a spirited relationship, with young Emily often giving as good as she got, both verbally and physically. Furious over his betrayal, Robiou turned Emily out of their home and told anyone who would listen, frequently and loudly, of his tribulation. Unfortunately, one place where he often launched into a verbal tirade was near the home of the Wormeley family, located off Robious Road near where Salisbury is today. In July 1851, having perhaps had enough of the loud disparaging of his daughter by her estranged husband, John Wormeley emerged from his home and shot Robiou, killing him instantly.

Wormeley was arrested, along with Reid, who was reported to have been present at the shooting. For the next two years, the scandal monopolized conversation around Chesterfield, with the acquittal of Reid, a mistrial declared due to a jury that had been supplied with alcohol by a deputy sheriff and the almost immediate marriage of young Emily to young Reid. An impartial jury could not be found from among Chesterfield residents, and jurors from Petersburg, Dinwiddie, Amelia and Richmond were brought in. After deliberating only for fifteen minutes, the jury found Wormeley guilty, and he was sentenced to hang. Four thousand spectators assembled at the Chesterfield jail on June 24, 1853. Wormeley asserted his daughter's innocence of infidelity, Reid's absence from the crime scene and Robiou's ill treatment of Emily to the crowd as he awaited his fate. Neither his wife nor his daughter was present to witness his hanging, and declaring, "Lord have mercy on my soul," Wormeley died. Barely rating a mention in accounts of the murder and subsequent trial through the decades is the child born to Robiou and Emily. Although he claimed that she was unfaithful to him, Robiou never asserted that his son was not his own. Not the least of the Robiou/Wormeley tragedies was the unexplained death of the infant, after someone "set his bed on fire" while Emily and her mother were at court.

This, however, was not to be the end to this macabre tale. In a slightly romanticized version, the young widow soon married Reid and, within two weeks, fell down the front stairs of the plantation home and died. Some claim that she fell on a sewing basket, impaling herself on a pair of scissors through the heart, and yet others say that she fell and broke her neck. It is said that both she and her murdered first husband Robiou occasionally return to the site of their tragedies. A number of people claim to have seen their apparitions in a boxwood garden behind the house. Today the site is home of the steakhouse, and many guests and employees have their own stories to tell. A more fact-driven conclusion to this dramatic saga is that Emily lived until sometime after 1860 and had three children: Samuel, Charles and Emma.

Louise Beattie

A Full and Complete History of the Great Beattie Case, Most Highly Sensational Tragedy of the Century, copyright 1911 by the Phoenix Publishing Company of Baltimore, tells the scandalous story of a notorious Chesterfield murder. Possibly due to the new technique enabling newspaper publishers to embed a photograph in the text of a story, the press was out in grand measure in the fall of 1911, screaming the story in bold headlines. Henry Beattie Jr., age twenty-six, son of a wealthy merchant and a man of considerable means himself, was taking his wife and four-month-old son to visit her family when he was supposedly set upon by a highwayman on Midlothian Turnpike. Mrs. Beattie was shot point-blank, but Mr. Beattie somehow escaped harm and drove his wife's lifeless body to the home of her uncle.

Beattie was arrested a few days later, and his story was torn apart by investigators, who could not reconcile his lack of wounds, the blood splatter patterns and the cryptic story of the purchase of a gun by Beattie that turned out to be the murder weapon. In the words of the Richmond newspaper of September 10, 1911: "Though even before the hands of the law were laid upon his shoulders, the world believed that Henry Beattie was the guilty man, and so said in general voice, the young husband had a fair trial. Every chance was afforded him to plead his cause. The law was allowed to take its course, for here in Virginia, it was believed that law would have its way." Motive? The handsome and debonair Henry Beattie had a secret life. Beulah Binford, aged seventeen, had met Beattie in 1907. Two years later, Beulah had given birth to a son by Beattie, named Henry Clay Beattie III. Soon afterward, she left the infant in the care of a relative while she pursued a baseball player in Martinsville. The child died within the year "of poor health."

Married to Louise Owen in 1910, Beattie soon after resumed intimacy with Beulah, meeting her in Norfolk. On May 31, 1911, son Henry Clay Beattie III was born to Beattie and his wife. Did Beulah give her married lover an ultimatum? We'll likely never know. What we do know is that in mid-July, Henry Beattie asked his cousin to buy him a shotgun and that the same gun was found at the murder scene days later. Meanwhile, the night before she was murdered, Louise was again being cheated on by Henry, who was with Beulah until well after midnight. Beattie was tried, convicted and executed on November 24, 1911. One of the most highly publicized crimes of the time, the Beattie murder was even featured in a tune written by country singer Kelly Harrel in 1927, who sang, "You don't confess that you killed her, you'll spend eternity in hell."

Some felt that the case against Beattie was based more on the illicit relationship than on the facts. Beattie himself laid the verdict on his relationship with Binford, declaring, "These country folks cannot understand how a woman of the underworld can be crazy about a man. They don't know when that happens how very hard it is to get rid of her." Not long after the verdict, mistress Binford and Beattie's cousin, Paul, were reported to be negotiating with a film magnate to do a movie/play about the case.

Phillip Tyler

A day of drinking and quarrelling apparently led to the slaying of Phillip Tyler of Winterpock, as reported in the Richmond newspaper of August 20, 1922. After listening to hours of disputes between his daughter and son-in-law, Charles Vaughan, Tyler, a preacher, inquired into the cause of the dispute. "None of your business what the trouble is," was Vaughan's reply. "I reckon you're right," responded Tyler, and he walked back down the stairs to his living area. At the bottom of the steps, Tyler was shot by Vaughan, who emptied a load of buckshot into his back and then reloaded the gun. Tyler died within fifteen minutes. Vaughan made no attempt to escape and "practically admitted to the shooting," as witnesses including his wife and her sister testified against him.

Detective Lyle B. Clements

Scrolling down the list of names on the Officer Down Memorial Page Inc. website, one can't help but be startled at the number of law enforcement officers who die each year in the line of duty. Detective Clements, aged twenty-five, was gunned down by a hobo in the Dunlop Freight Yards in Chesterfield on September 3, 1930, while on duty. The suspect had shot another railroad police officer the week before in North Carolina. Detective Clements found the hobo in a coal car on a train and attempted to arrest him. Armed with a handgun, the hobo shot Clements four times. Clements was able to shoot back, hitting the suspect in the leg, before being thrown off the train. The suspect was found, captured and sentenced to life in prison for the murder of the young officer.

Fred, Lucy and Cristle Sue Hofer

At a quiet country farm site in Moseley, honeysuckle was in the air and the lowing of cows whispered through the June evening as Chesterfield detectives searched the crime scene at Criswood, home of Fred and Lucille Hofer and their fifteen-year-old daughter, Cristle Sue. The 1962 slaying of the Hofer family stunned this farming community, located just six miles north of Hull Street Road. The Hofers' sixteen-year-old hired hand, Hubert Templeton, was apprehended later that night on the Skyline Drive after a fifteen-state alert was broadcast for Templeton, driving the Hofers' car.

The Hofers had last been seen shopping at Southside Plaza that Friday afternoon. Sue, as the daughter was called, had been dismissed from school

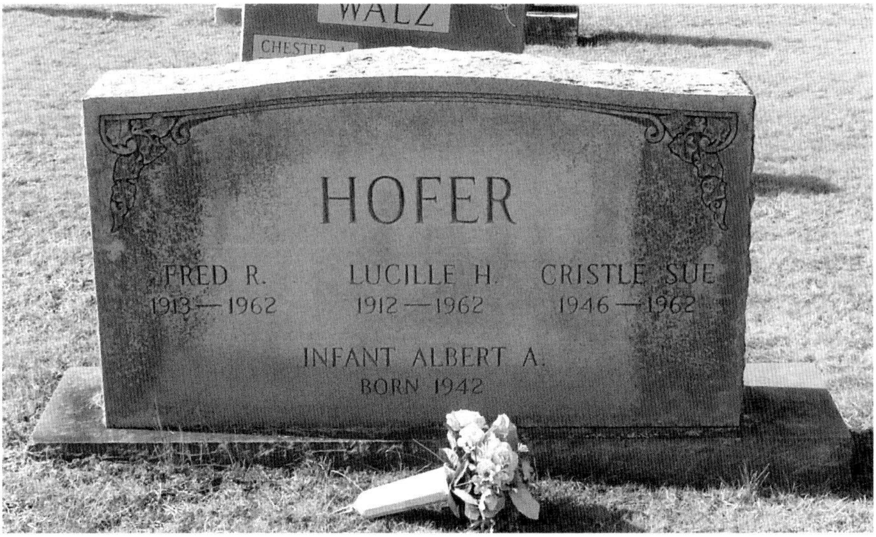

A Hofer tombstone at Mount Hermon cemetery. *Cemetery Committee, CHSV.*

early to go shopping with her parents. Her school, Grange Hall, was having its annual awards program that night, and Sue was to play the clarinet in the program. Her blood-spattered white hair bow was found near her body. She had been shot multiple times and was found in a utility shed. Her parents were also shot and left in the yard of their home. The house had been ransacked.

Templeton was a troubled youth, running away from home many times, as well as from a school in which he had been placed in New Jersey and Oak Hill Academy in Virginia. More than once he had lived in the woods or in the school buildings during vacations rather than going home. Pastor M.K. Roberson of Ridge Baptist Church had helped arrange for the troubled boy to live in the country, on a farm with the Hofers, who reportedly treated him well, even giving him allowances. Roberson reported in the June 3, 1962 edition of the *Richmond Times-Dispatch* that Mrs. Hofer "knew the boy's record from A to Z…[and] had one thing in mind—to give him a home. She understood as I did that the boy needed to adjust to the world he lives in." Templeton admitted to the killing, stating that his reason for killing the Hofers was that Mrs. Hofer nagged him too much.

The Hofers are buried at Mount Hermon Baptist Church. Templeton was convicted of three counts of capital murder and served many years in the penitentiary, where he died.

Murder and mayhem; liquor and lust; temper, temptation, intolerance and transgression—Chesterfield tragedies, buried in time, with only newspaper headlines and cemetery stones to tell the sad story of lives destroyed by human vice. Yesterday was not so different from today.

The Women of Matoaca Mills

We normally think of our part of the South as being a slave-based agricultural economy, but in the years preceding the Civil War, industrialization developed to support the plantation system, with its need for mills, railroads and ironworks. Throughout the southern countryside, manufacturing facilities were established.

The small village along the north bank of the Appomattox River known as Matoaca began as a mill town in the 1830s. Named for the daughter of Powhatan—who was known more formally as Pocahontas—the village was strategically located at the terminus of the canal locks of the Upper Appomattox Company, which provided good passage for the raw cotton from North Carolina. The village's proximity to Petersburg, with its port and rail centers, made the location of mills at Matoaca practical. The Matoaca Manufacturing Company operated gristmills and manufactured paper in addition to cotton.

Before the Civil War, farm families were largely self-sufficient and produced a variety of fruits, vegetables, grain and livestock, but following the war, many small farmers fell deeply in debt, and mill work provided an opportunity for economic stability and to fund rebuilding. This income could help keep a farm running and support the family. Children, particularly daughters, were not very useful on the farm and had much more value to their families as millworkers.

Many different business enterprises flourished in Chesterfield in the mixed industrial and agricultural economy after the war, including coal mining, tanneries and canneries, ironworks and brickyards. The Matoaca textile mill, constructed circa 1836, contained four thousand spindles and 170 looms. A village of fifteen to twenty tenement houses was the genesis of a settlement that grew to about five hundred people. In late nineteenth-century Matoaca, white women were a substantial part of the workforce. Black workers would have been less expensive, but the culture dictated that only white labor was employed in the South's cotton mills. Men held positions as managers, mechanics, clerks and packers, while women worked as spinners, carders and weavers.

The female workers at the Matoaca mill created female bonds, or networks, in the workplace by sharing daily work routines and responsibilities. The majority of these women were not married; still, they faced the same double duty that today's working women face, as they left the workplace after a ten- to twelve-hour shift for the "second shift" at home. They worked six days a week, and in the pre-Christmas months, thirteen- to fourteen-hour shifts were common. Lacking today's appliances, the work at home was much more labor-intensive and tedious.

Matoaca's working mill women formed networks based on their roles in the community, home and workplace, as women traditionally do. These networks served the purpose of sharing family obligations, as well as providing work exchanges whereby women could provide for their work replacement should they need to take time off work. This arrangement helped both the temporary worker who became known to potential employers and the worker who needed time off without having the fear of losing her job.

The women's networks shared with one another whenever they could, with whatever energy they had left over. They were expanded to include neighbors, coworkers and church friends. Leisure time was never abundant and always took second place to obligations to family and community. Unscheduled mill

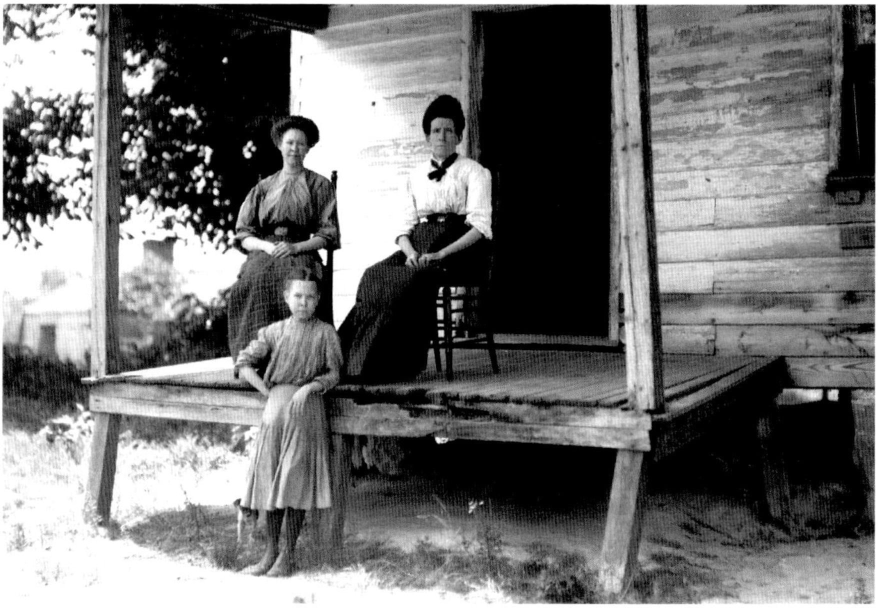

Mrs. Fannie Foster, a widow who worked in the Matoaca mills, and her daughters in 1911. *Library of Congress, records of the National Child Labor Committee.*

stoppages and Sunday and holiday closings provided opportunities for outings in the country or fishing excursions. Events known as "work-sharings" had a long tradition in rural communities and were used by women to can and preserve, quilt and make wine and cider, while the men shared in the work to harvest crops, clear ground and raise barns. These gatherings got the work done at the same time that they united the community and provided entertainment.

Proper and acceptable behavior—or reprimands for improper and unacceptable behavior—was defined or doled out by the female networks, and religious services provided a major outlet for the women of Matoaca. Guest preachers, prayer meetings and multiple Sunday services were occasions that combined religion and entertainment. Much of the church social activity centered on matchmaking, with games designed to pair couples up. Often, social matches were made known to the community in this setting. Church-sponsored community dating was part of the Matoaca female culture, and weddings were special social events. The experiences and values shared, along with the responsibilities and duties required in the industrial setting, helped form a postwar southern female culture that carried through into the early years of the twentieth century, when "labor militancy" actively involved southern women in pursuing collective goals through social and political means.

Chesterfield's Ghostly Past

It seems there is a renewed interest in our county's history lately. Perhaps kindled by the 2007 celebrations of the 400th birthday of our nation at Jamestown and spurred by the upcoming sesquicentennial of the Civil War, longtime citizens in addition to our county's newest residents are intrigued by stories of Chesterfield's past. Many people from all across the country can trace their roots all the way back to the original settlers who landed at Jamestown and wandered up the river to settle Henricus, Bermuda Hundred and points west. They say that there's nothing new under the sun, and the following stories illustrate the scandals and folktales that survive from earlier Chesterfield days. See what details you can recognize from these stories.

Wrexham Hall's Lady in Red

The closest neighbor to Castlewood (home of the Chesterfield Historical Society of Virginia) used to be Wrexham Hall, formerly known as the Goode House. The house has since been moved three-quarters of a mile from the

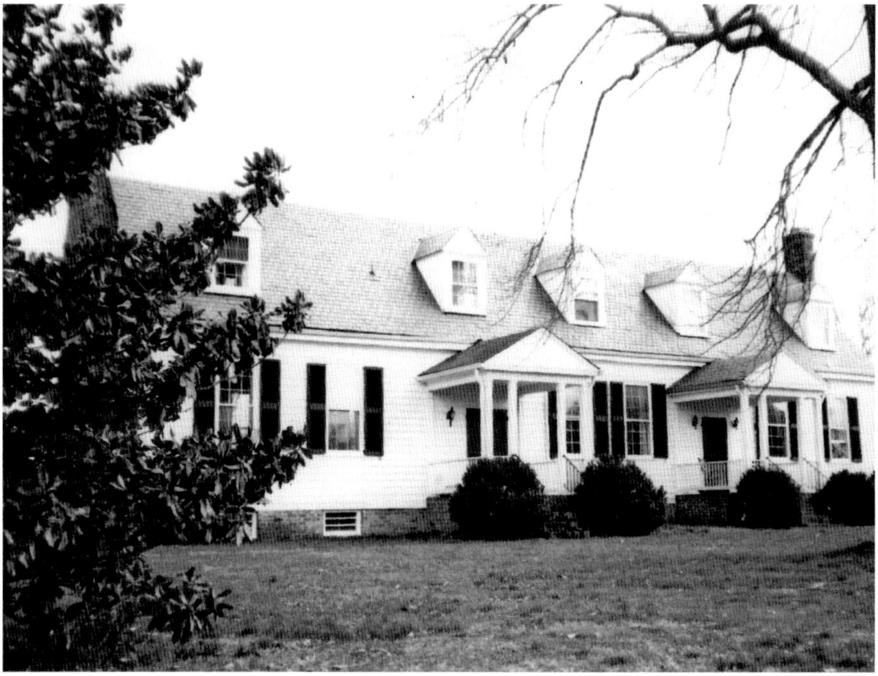

Wrexham Hall in 1983. Built by Archibald Walthall about 1750, the house is believed to be haunted. *Chesterfield Historical Society of Virginia.*

courthouse area to a new subdivision called Wrexham Estates, just northeast of Iron Bridge and Centralia Roads, a property originally belonging to Archibald Walthall. It is a unique structure now, composed of parts of two houses. One wing is actually an older wing of another home called Fruit Hill that was an addition acquired for its period flooring and added on to the original house. Wrexham Hall derived its name from a village in Wales from which a former owner's ancestors originated.

The specter at Wrexham Hall deserves special attention and is quite unusual, for it centers on a "Lady Dressed in Red." When Archibald Walthall died, the property was willed to his daughter, Susannah. It was eventually sold with one stipulation: that a certain plot of land containing the family graveyard was to be reserved for the family. John Goode purchased the property in 1830 and built the current house. The property was sold several times during the nineteenth century.

One of the owners, Stanley Hague, spotted the apparition only once while working outside in the field across from Wrexham Hall. He noticed a woman dressed in red sitting on the front porch. No explanation was ever found for the vision. Some say that it was the ghost of Susannah Walthall looking for her lost headstone. While the lady has never been *seen* again, she has made her presence known on a regular basis, from footsteps on the stairs to rocking chairs that appear to rock in the night. People left alone in the house feel the presence of someone else in the room with them. Family articles that disappear and later reappear, doors that open and close unexpectedly and occasional inexplicable cold gusts of air that burst suddenly through rooms are other unexplained occurrences at Wrexham.

Who is this mysterious lady, why does she haunt Wrexham Hall and why is she dressed in red? Many of the previous owners have not been able to determine the answers to any of these questions. Could it be the spirit of Susannah Walthall, who has remained at Wrexham all these years still searching for her long-lost family graveyard? Today, Susannah's and the rest of the grave sites are commemorated in a spot in the middle of the Martin's Supermarket parking lot, protected by some attractive landscaping and part of the day-to-day life in Chesterfield County.

The Mystique of Physic Hill

One of the more puzzling reports of phenomena has come from a house located off Winterpock Road in Chesterfield County known as Physic Hill. There have been numerous reports of hauntings and an ethereal presence over a period of many years. Occupants of the house have reported strange goings-on, such as lights flickering on and off for no apparent reason. Lights upstairs would dim and then come back on to their full brilliance. Pictures hanging on the walls would mysteriously fall to the floor. They would be hung back on the wall only to be found on the floor again the next time one entered a room. Later, the sound of footsteps could be heard over the top of the master bedroom. They were real, not imagined, so claim the owners of the house.

One especially odd occurrence was finding the bed in the upstairs guest room taken completely apart, with the mattress on the floor. No broken or loose parts could be found. It was as if something or someone was not satisfied with the way the house had been decorated and was venting its frustration. Yet other incidents have been cited, from encountering no hot water from certain faucets in the house to draperies found lying on the floor, which couldn't be explained.

Physic Hill is a historic plantation in the Winterpock area of the county. Dr. John Walke, a physician from Amelia County, built the house in two stages in 1815. The second side-passage wing was added in 1825. The present basement was once a root cellar, where it is rumored that Dr. Walke would incarcerate and discipline unruly slaves on his plantation. It is also believed that slaves were brought to this location to be examined by the doctor before being sold at public auction. The house was named for a succession of physicians who lived in the house over the years.

Dr. Walke married Martha Branch from Willow Hill. The Walke family graveyard is located southeast of the house, and one headstone, within sight of the upstairs bedroom, is inscribed with the name "Martha Walke." It is the only marked stone on the plantation, and it is believed that the spirit that haunts the house is that of Martha.

Why her spirit haunts Physic Hill is unknown. Not much is known about her death. She might have died violently—and that is why she returns. On the other hand, she possibly could be angry with her husband, who married twice after her death, each time bringing his new bride to Physic Hill. One interesting sidebar to this story is that a painting of John Walke owned by one of his descendants was found by the owners of the house. It was photographed and hung over the fireplace. For a short time, this seemed to appease the spirits, but they eventually started up once again.

The Winged Harbinger of Death

What we now know as Clover Hill plantation has been described as one of the most historically significant plantations in Chesterfield County. The house is believed to have been constructed in 1787, beginning with the large two-story section. Two other sections were built shortly after the Civil War, and various one-story additions have been added since. The house was built by the Cox family; James H. Cox moved to the farm known as Winterpock in 1835. Sometime shortly after that, his wife changed the name to Clover Hill. A rich vein of coal was discovered on the property, giving rise to the Clover Hill Coal Mines that prospered during the 1800s. The coal was carried to the James River on the Clover Hill Railroad.

Many stories have been passed down by former slaves and others concerning Clover Hill. Many of these strange tragedies have become classic ghost stories. These include tales of birds flying through the house as a prelude to death, eerie rappings on doors of the house before a family member's impending death and phantoms and banshees soaring through skeletal branches of the once glorious Lombardy poplars, as well as mysterious deaths.

The most intriguing Clover Hill story deals with the great blizzard of 1857, which has become known by Chesterfield County residents as "Cox's Snow." Dr. Joseph Cox, a cousin of Henry's, was called from his home to visit a patient one cold evening in January 1857. He drove his horse and buggy through the snow to see his patient and decided to return home, even though it was late at night. The trip back was long and slow, but he made it to the front gate of Clover Hill, frozen to the bone. He fought his way through the drifts of snow to unlatch the front gate, which was icy and frozen shut. He frantically called out for help in the driving snowstorm, but no one could hear his pleas. The next morning, slaves found Dr. Cox out near the front gate, frozen to death and holding on to the gate leading up to his own front porch.

According to former slaves, strange things began happening at Clover Hill following this event, mostly occurring in the upstairs bedroom, where something (or someone) keeps watch in a most discomforting manner. Many believe that it is the ghost of frozen Dr. Cox. He will not let whoever is sleeping in the room keep any bedcovers on them. Another Clover Hill story involves the cedars that now line the carriage drive where poplars once stood. Before the Civil War, slaves believed that a headless horseman rode among the trees at night. They made such a fuss that Judge Cox had the trees cut down.

Then there were the gruesome stories of the spring from which fresh water was drawn for the house. There have been accounts of slaves who were found mutilated near the spring. Some of these stories are legend, but one account has been partially documented. It describes a slave who was sent down to the well to draw water and was later found with his or her head and torso in the water. The story is split as to the gender of the slave and includes the possibility that he or she was killed by an overseer. Afterward, no one would go down to the well for water, even under the threat of punishment. Subsequently, the spring was bricked up and never used again.

Several members of the Cox family have died suddenly at Clover Hill—each time, according to servants, preceded by a harbinger of death, taking the form of a sharp rapping against a particular side door of the house. There have been numerous occurrences of a swooping bird that made a sign of death. During the Civil War, James Cox was relaxing in his study one evening. His three sons had joined the Confederate army, and he was alone in the room. He heard a fluttering of wings and observed a dark bird circling above his head that then flew out the window. Shortly afterward, Mr. Cox and his wife made a trip to Norfolk to visit their youngest son where he was stationed. They found their boy very ill and brought him back to Clover Hill, where his health grew worse. He died the day after Christmas and was laid out in the parlor where the bird had appeared. The Coxes called the death after the appearance of the bird a coincidence; however, the servants had another name for it: they called it "hants."

Mysteries at Castlewood

Stories have abounded surrounding the historic house known as Castlewood located on Iron Bridge and Krause Roads. The house is a fine example of Federal-style architecture. The central section was built in 1816. The northern wing is an eighteenth-century building moved from another part of the property. The original builder of the house was Parke Poindexter, who served as the clerk of the Chesterfield County Court from 1812 through 1849, so the building would have been used for receptions and court business.

Strange phenomena have been said to take place over the years, involving doors being unlocked and items being moved around over night. It is believed that the spirit of Mr. Poindexter or some of his guests still haunt Castlewood.

Magnolia Grange House Museum Mystery

Magnolia Grange is a lovely gem of a Federal-style home built in 1822 by William Winfree. Winfree's wife, Lucy, is believed to be the graceful spirit who very rarely makes an appearance on the steps at the Grange. Although the county-owned building is visited by thousands of tourists every year and is frequently the site of social gatherings for county officials and private citizens renting it for special occasions, in only three instances have people allegedly observed the lovely lady on the steps, and all three describe her in the same way: pretty, petite and blonde, with her hair pinned up in the back and ringlets framing her face, the woman wears an empire-style white gown and a serene, welcoming smile.

Following a small wedding early in 2010, the groom mentioned to a family member that there had been a woman in period costume who stood at the bottom of the steps and, making eye contact with him, smiled as she turned and walked up the stairs. Intrigued by this report and not having seen any such person herself, a relative of the groom phoned the docent at Magnolia Grange and inquired about the costumed interpreter who had been upstairs. She was informed that there had not been such a person there that day.

Truth…or merely our imaginations looking for expression to enliven our lives? Who knows? The oral traditions among slaves and illiterate settlers surely become embellished over time, and everyone loves a good ghost story—if it is "just a story" at all.

Part III
VILLAGES

BON AIR: CHESTERFIELD'S EARLY RESORT DESTINATION

Today, if one were to go to the intersection of Buford and Rockaway Roads in northwestern Chesterfield, he would be at the center of what was, in the late 1870s, a wonderful Victorian resort village. The city of Richmond was thriving at the turn of the twentieth century, and suburbs began to develop in areas like Bon Air, Chester and Midlothian. Bon Air, with its quaint Victorian nature, is a favorite of many metropolitan-area residents today. This village retains some of the aura of the early days, with shops that fill specialty niches and a definite attitude among residents that they are living in an area rich with local color and history.

In the mid-1800s, summer resorts were popular among people with disposable means. The tidewater regions had threats of malaria, along with high temperatures and humidity, and residents escaped to places like White Sulphur Springs. In the early 1870s, a group of businessmen thought it would be a good idea to build a resort closer to Richmond. Along the line of the Richmond and Danville Railroad was a spot with higher elevation featuring woodland and farms: Brown's Summit. The Bon Air Land and Improvement Company of Virginia, composed of these businessmen, was formed in 1877. The goal was to create a resort village with improved land, streets, roads and lanes. The officers of the Richmond and Danville Railroad quickly recognized an opportunity to make money, and they agreed to build a depot in the resort area, as well as to give owners reduced shipping rates for building supplies and commuter fares.

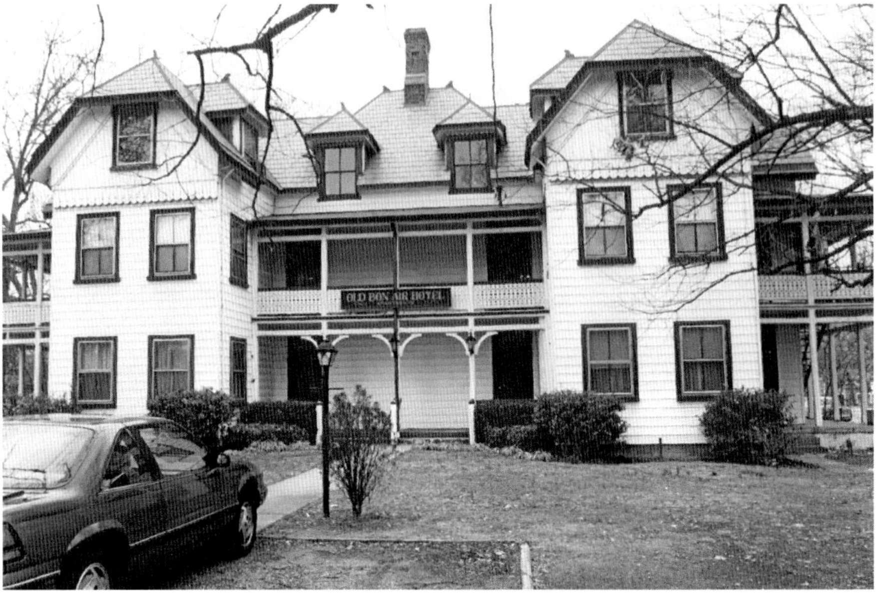

The Bon Air Hotel annex, consisting of twenty rooms, was added to the original hotel in 1881. The main hotel burned in 1889 and was never reconstructed. *Chesterfield Historical Society of Virginia.*

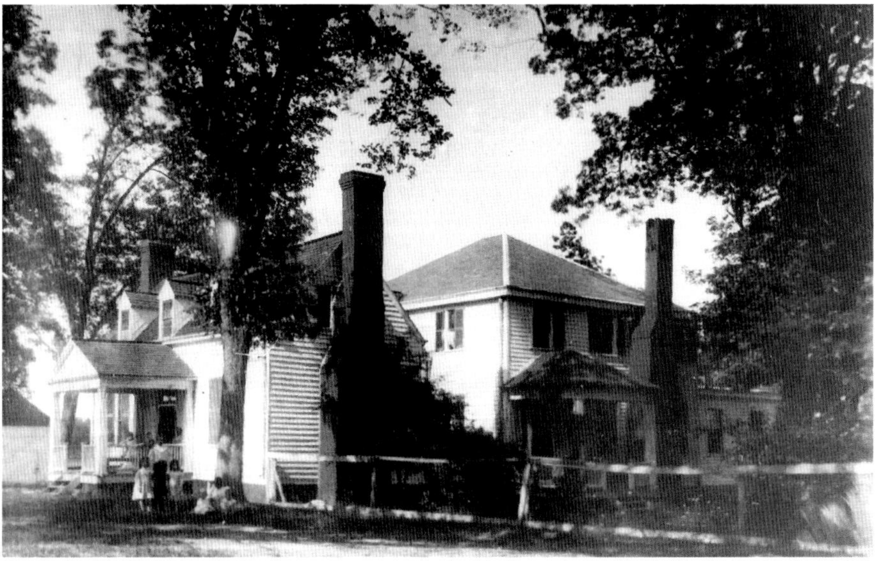

Kilbourne, Bon Air, the home of Benjamin F. Johnson and family, photo circa 1895. *Chesterfield Historical Society of Virginia.*

The Bon Air Hotel was the first building erected in the budding village, in 1880. It was a large three-story wood-frame building with public rooms, thirty-six guest rooms, verandas, grounds landscaped with riding trails, croquet and lawn tennis courts, archery ranges, baseball fields and even a field for jousting. A males-only bowling alley and billiard room was located in a separate building erected soon after. The public immediately became interested in these luxurious accommodations with the proposed village surrounding, and 178 lots were sold or leased very quickly.

The first seasons were such a success that the Bon Air Hotel added a twenty-room annex in 1880–81 and a church (Bon Air Christian Church) the year after. Five years later, "the Steps" were erected—an elaborate wooden staircase with multiple platforms built into the hillside beside the railroad tracks. Trains made the trek between Richmond five times daily and excursion runs once each weeknight. The cars could be rented for private parties, and church and civic groups brought their members out for picnics and day parties. Some families rented suites at the hotel for the entire summer, while others built summer "cottages" along the well-laid-out streets of Bon Air.

The Bon Air Hotel burned to the ground in 1889, and the nature of the village changed. The hotel's poor insurance coverage precluded rebuilding, and the resort immediately suffered. A smaller inn was built, but without the rooms and the social amenities of the old resort, and the village evolved into a commuter village. This change was facilitated by the improvement in sanitary conditions in the city and the successful streetcar system opening in Richmond in 1888, which extended out to Bon Air. An 1896 survey listed thirty households, and Bon Air remained a close-knit village community populated by railroad executives, war veterans and business executives. One well-known resident was George S. Cook, one of America's most popular photographers, and it is due to his resources that we have a very complete visual record of life in Bon Air before the turn of the century.

The year 1917 brought the end of the resort era with the closing of the Bon Air Hotel and the cessation of rail service, but Bon Air saw other kinds of growth. After the Second World War, subdivisions and shopping centers sprouted up in the area, and it is now part of the larger Richmond/Chesterfield metropolitan region. Efforts by the Bon Air Historical Society and others dedicated to preserving the community's unique past and individuality have been rewarded recently by the finding of maps of the village from 1921, showing its large lots, grand houses and multiple outbuildings. The society has established the annual Bon Air Victorian Day celebration, a charitable fundraising event popular throughout the area, held each year in May.

EARLY SUBURBS OF CHESTERFIELD COUNTY

Suburbs of Richmond, Virginia, began to develop in the early years of the twentieth century as commuter rail and the automobile made living outside of the commercial and business area feasible.

Manufacturers and wealthy merchants built quasi-estates in the Manchester area and around the Appomattox River, and Richmond had a class of prominent businessmen who built estates south of the city that are considered huge by today's standards. As transportation became readily accessible, the practice of having a country estate in addition to a townhouse transitioned into the establishment of single, large landholdings—most of these were built along main transportation routes such as the Richmond and Petersburg Electric Railway, which had fifteen stops, with trolleys arriving and departing every half hour. By the 1920s and 1930s, most of the population growth of the urban area was coming from outside the city limits.

Homes were built back then in a wider range of styles than we are used to seeing in suburbia today. Colonial, craftsman and bungalow styles were popular and were either built by local architects or adapted from plans by popular nationally known architects, or they were by plans purchased from mail-order firms.

Several decades earlier, however, Chesterfield County already had some settlements that could have been considered suburbs. A well-known example was the village of Bon Air; another is the area of Meadowbrook. Some of the dwellings in this area were on a scale unlike anything else in the Chesterfield area.

Miniborya is an Indian word meaning "falling water," and it was one of the large dwellings in the Meadowbrook area, on the west side of Falling Creek. Built in 1899–1900, it stood only until 1973, when the Meadowbrook apartments were built on its site. The architectural style of the dwelling was a composite of traditional styles and featured gables, dormers, a gambrel roof, a three-sided veranda and even a tower. It was the grounds, however, that formed the sensational aspect of this particular estate. The owner, J. Scott Parrish, was the founder of Concrete Pipe and Products Company, and his grounds were landscaped extravagantly with terraces, parterres and graveled walkways. Greenhouses, barns and guest cottages were also features of this estate.

Theodore Page was a northerner who built a home called Argyle in 1906. The property has a current-day view of the Meadowbrook golf course and the James River Valley. An early example of Colonial Revival style, it featured wonderful gables, dormers and pavilions. When nearby Meadowbrook estate burned to the ground in 1913, its owner, Thomas Jeffress, bought Argyle to live in for six years while the replacement home was built at Meadowbrook. James Hening—prominent school board member, founder and president of the Chesterfield County Fair and member of the board of supervisors—purchased Argyle in 1919 and lived there until his death in 1953. The Meadowbrook Country Club took ownership of the house in 1957, and in the mid-1960s, it was sold again to private owners.

Today's Meadowbrook Country Clubhouse sits on part of what was once a 3,000-acre tobacco plantation. A twenty-six-room Tudor-style mansion, its beginnings were much more modest: a frame building surrounded by gardens that burned in 1913. The builder, Thomas Jeffress, had a wife who was a master gardener and who guided professional landscapers in creating a spectacular showplace. Twin teahouses were one of the features of this well-known garden, which Mrs. Jeffress hoped to eventually open to the public, much like the present day Maymont gardens. Meadowbrook was a working farm, with angus cattle, grapevines and tobacco, until 1957, when a group of Richmond and Chesterfield businessmen purchased the house and 220 acres of land from a North Carolinian to whom Thomas Jeffress had sold it. This was the founding of the Meadowbrook Country Club until the structure, like its precursor, burned to the ground in 1967.

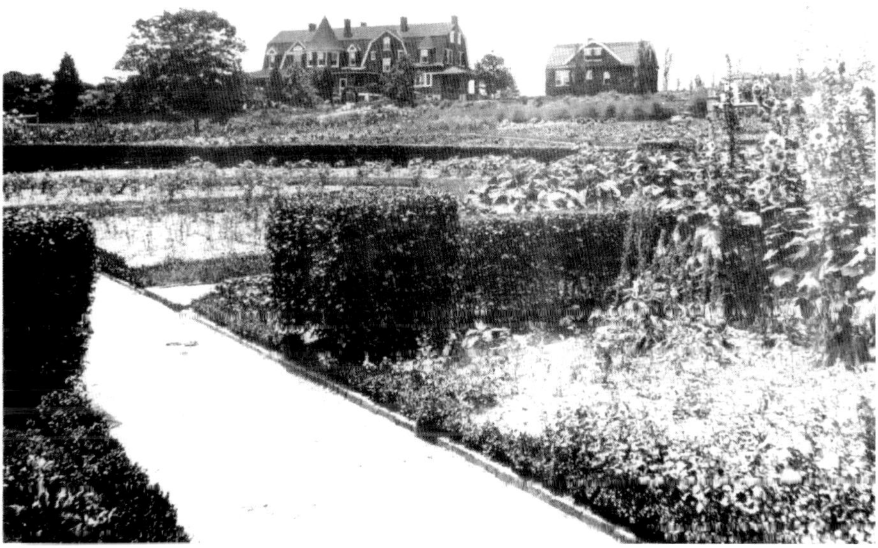

Miniborya. *Cook Collection, Valentine Richmond History Center.*

Sources report that in spite of the fantastic estates in the young suburb of Meadowbrook, the natural beauty in the area was Falling Creek, before the building of the dam on Hopkins Road in 1951. A favorite spot for picnics, the creek was shaded by beech trees and featured huge slabs of granite as places on which to rest and eat.

WINTERPOCK AND CLOVER HILL

Many families arrived in America via the seaport at Bermuda Hundred. Among them, in 1621, was the Shippy family. Martha, a daughter in this family, married a successful planter in what was then Henrico, had several children, was widowed in her late thirties or early forties and went on to become one of Chesterfield's earliest land developers. The property that Martha Stratton patented, along with eight other investors, was described as being "below the mouth of the Wintopock creek," a name believed to be derived from the Indian name for the creek, *Win-to-poa-ke*.

The land was separated, and upon her death, Martha willed four hundred acres at "Wontopork" to her grandson, Henry Cox. His son, also named Henry, was born in the area and was the first to build on the land, in about 1775. The second Henry Cox was politically active in Chesterfield and signed the petition to dissolve the Convention of Virginia in 1775, following the British acts of aggression.

The unique home built by Henry was located on a hillside, overlooking the creek, and was an English-style cottage consisting of two rooms on the first floor and two small bedrooms on the upper half-story. Shortly thereafter, a second structure was added, with a large square room on the first floor and a second-floor bedroom. Henry Cox had another home near Goode's Bridge and gave Winterpock plantation to his second son, James, in 1834. James achieved fame as a member of the Virginia House of Delegates, as a senator representing Chesterfield and Petersburg and as a delegate of the Constitutional Convention from the Petersburg District. He was later president of the Secession Convention, the owner of the Winterpock mines and the first county judge in Chesterfield County. James Cox's wife, Martha Reid, renamed the plantation Clover Hill, after the slopes of green clover surrounding the main house, and it is thus known today.

In the year 1837, legend has it that a slave named Moses found coal on the land following a heavy rain, and this important discovery led to the operation of several mines at Clover Hill. The Clover Hill Railroad was

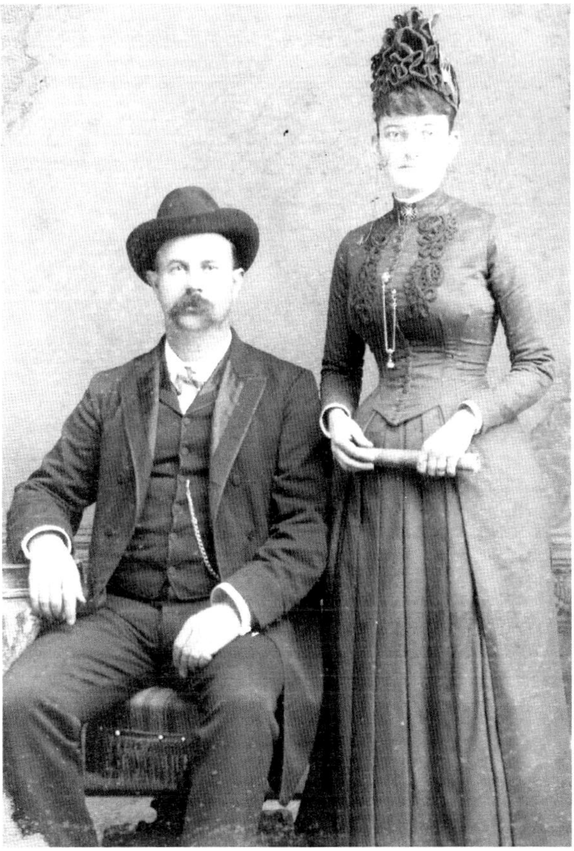

Mr. and Mrs. John H. Cox of Clover Hill, 1890. They were the parents of Virginia Cox Tucker, the last of the Cox families to live at Clover Hill. *Chesterfield Historical Society of Virginia.*

built in the 1840s to haul Cox's coal to Manchester, where it was loaded onto steamships bound for the gasworks in New York and Philadelphia. The name Winterpock was later applied to the mining community that grew up a mile from the house. This community peaked at about one thousand residents in the 1870s but dwindled down considerably when the mines closed late in the nineteenth century.

Judge James Cox died in 1877 following his son, who died on the battlefield at Appomattox. The plantation remained in Cox family hands until the 1920s.

Two noteworthy incidents add dramatic layers to the rich pedigree of this home, which is lovingly occupied today. In January 1857, during one of the worst recorded snowstorms in Virginia history—now referred to as "Cox's Snow"—Dr. Edwin Cox, a brother of Judge Cox, froze to death at the entrance to Clover Hill. He was stranded in the snow while returning to his home plantation north of Clover Hill after seeing a patient in Petersburg.

At the gate to Clover Hill, both he, his companion and their horse were overcome by the cold a mere seven hundred yards from the house.

In her book *My Confederate Girlhood*, Kate Virginia Cox Logan, a daughter of James Cox, recalled the brief visit of General Robert E. Lee to Clover Hill on April 2, 1865, during the Southern army's retreat to Appomattox. Kate, a young woman at that time, wrote:

> *General Lee's…time for being with us was short…but before dinner could be placed on the table, there was a brief interval…to me belonged the privilege of a short talk with General Lee, which incident is written on my memory never to be effaced. I said, "General Lee, we shall still gain our cause; you will join General Johnston and together you will be victorious." My poor little attempt at sympathy—breathing hope, was met with: "Whatever happens, know this, that no men ever fought better than those who have stood by me."*

The Clover Hill plantation house has been home to many, many families, both free and slave. Several outbuildings surrounded it, including one that may have been Clover Hill Academy, a conservatory at which oranges and

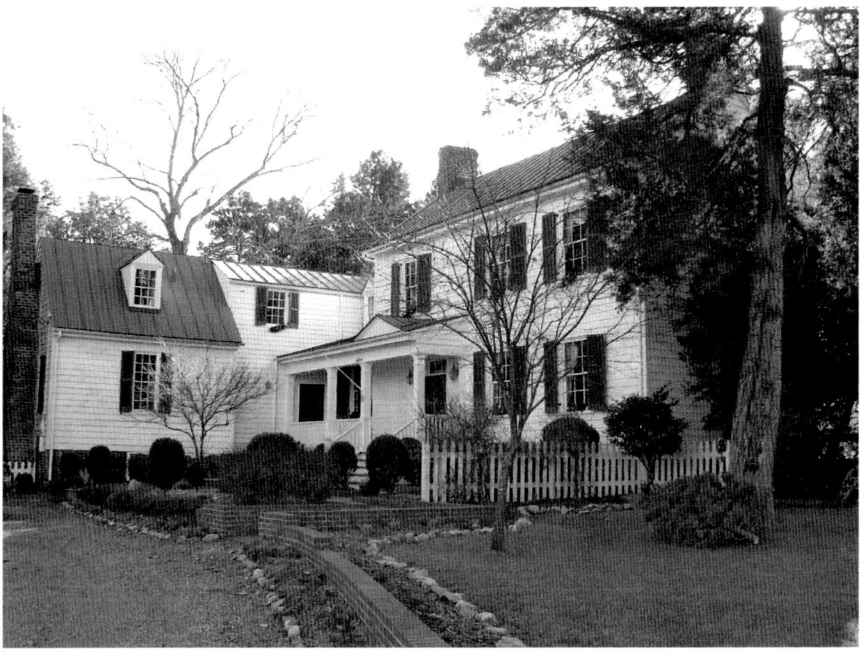

Clover Hill. *Rachel Lipowicz.*

lemons were grown, and slave and servant quarters, most of which no longer survive. The property passed from Cox family hands in the 1920s, and the home has been carefully renovated. Many other stories, some featuring tales of hauntings, enrich the fascinating narrative of the Clover Hill plantation house, making it one of the shiniest gems of Chesterfield's historic past.

Screamersville

The year 1865 brought an end to slavery in Chesterfield County, as children learn in elementary school. What happened to former slaves at that point is not as well known. As they were considered to be valuable personal property, slave records mostly exist as parts of last wills and testaments, and most of today's African American citizens in our county have a very difficult time tracing their family roots.

One of the areas believed to have been settled by former slaves was at the southeastern end of the county and was called Screamersville. Consisting at its peak of fewer than one hundred residents, little remains of this area today. Many houses were torn down in the 1980s as construction of Interstate 295 was completed, and residents had been moving out of the area since the 1960s in pursuit of educational and career opportunities.

Possibly named for its fondness for partying, Screamersville had a reputation for bootlegging during prohibition days. Dancing in the yards was a favorite pastime. Police officers in the area were frequently called out there to quiet things down. However, by the time the police would arrive at the purported scene of commotion, everyone had known that they were coming and things quite often had settled down on their own. Relationships between residents and the police were cordial—the residents understood that the police had a job to do, and the officers understood the extreme poverty that led residents to party with passion on occasion. Most Screamersville inhabitants worked in a nearby sawmill, and the work was hard and paid little. Children attended a one-room school for blacks that was located three or four miles away and to which they had to walk.

Screamersville residents were a close-knit group who cared for and looked after one another. Some claimed that the community's name actually came from the constant communication from front porch to front porch before telephones were commonplace. Four graveyards were located in the settlement, and another popular theory is that the screaming for which it is named is due to the sounds coming from them. John Strachan, a white

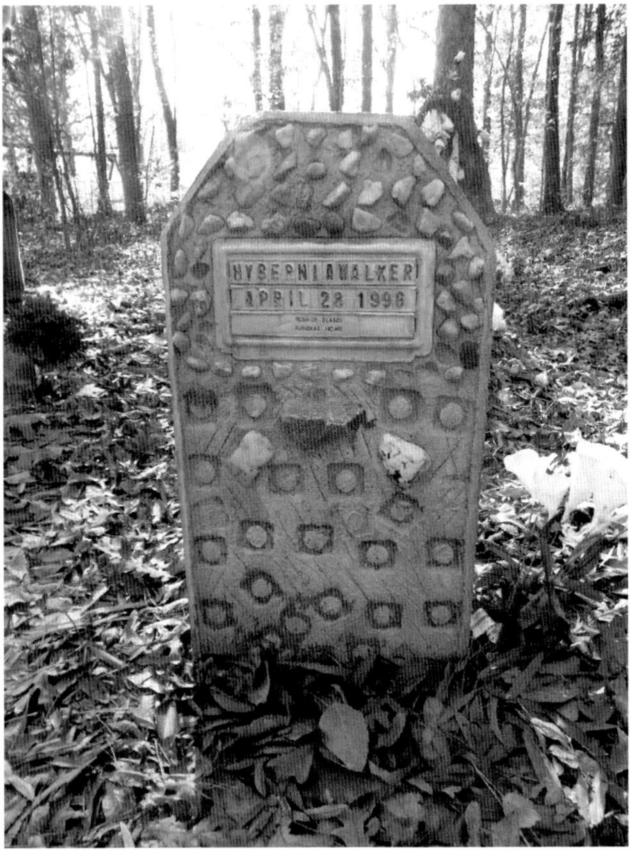

This homemade gravestone, embellished with pebbles, memorializes Hybernia Walker in the Walker cemetery in Screamersville. *Cemetery Committee, CHSV.*

man, founded Enon Baptist Church in 1849. He owned much of the land that evolved into Screamersville, including 375 acres that he inherited from his father, who moved there in 1813. The Strachan cemetery is one of the four within the boundaries of the original settlement. Now surrounded by twentieth-century development, the graves and their "screaming" inhabitants are about all that remain today of the little community with the unique name.

HALLSBOROUGH: A NINETEENTH-CENTURY COMMUNITY

Once upon a time, Chesterfield was a network of small communities, each with its own flavor, personality and purpose. Often situated beside a railway, these communities were not far apart by today's standards, but in the days when traveling twenty miles on horseback took half a day, they had a distinct "separateness" about them.

We have a map that we use often in the library of the Chesterfield Historical Society of Virginia called the *LaPrade Map of 1888*. Compiled from the census of 1880 and "made by order of the Board of Supervisors" by surveyor J.E. LaPrade, this interesting map shows the homesteads and landmarks within the communities of the county, many of which we still know today. The population of Chesterfield was then 18,044, and the county was composed of 296,451 acres. It was divided into two districts: the First District covered Manchester, Midlothian and Bermuda, and the Second District included Clover Hill, Dale and Matoaca.

A small area just east of the Powhatan line and north of Swift Creek was known as Hallsboro, or Hallsborough (the differing names can allegedly be traced to hurt feelings from when the post office was relocated in later years). A map examiner will note that there are several homesteads marked on the LaPrade map, as well as the Hallsboro Station and tannery. Most of Chesterfield today is not familiar with this area of the county, but the Hallsborough Tavern stands as a monument to the mid- and late-nineteenth century life in this area.

The original section of the Hallsborough Tavern might have been constructed as early as late eighteenth century, and subsequent additions were made about 1832 and 1890. The earliest owner of the tract was Daniel W. Michaux, a Huguenot descendant. In 1810, James Howard bought the land and established a tavern and retail merchandise store. When he died in 1822, his 1,400 acres and buildings were valued at $2,866. The next owner, Austin Spears, continued the operation of the tavern and made the enlargements in 1832 that allowed him to house more travelers. The Lynchburg stagecoach stopped there daily, and the tavern also functioned as a post office. There were stables for the stage and patrons' horses, as well as an equipment shop for them on the property.

The area began to grow and consisted of several dwelling houses, a large Baptist church, the tavern and store and a school. Schools in those days were "old field" schools, or community schools, so named because they were often built on land that could no longer be farmed. In Chesterfield, only about 20 percent of the nonslave school-aged children attended any kind of school, despite the availability of government subsidies, and the level of education accessible ranged from secondary to barely rudimentary. Not shown on the LaPrade map, the schoolhouse at Hallsboro had originally been built as a cottage for a mill foreman. Mr. Thomas E. Marshall was the teacher—a man with a Phi Beta Kappa key from Hampton Sydney College. Students sat on benches with no back and used planks attached to the wall for desks.

Taverns were social centers for a community and served as anything from a one-room public meeting space to a multiple-room hotel. Some were private homes where families rented out rooms to travelers. Most taverns, whatever their form, served a vital function as communications centers for the community. Business deals were forged there, peddlers found customers there and games and sports events took place there, as well as card and dice games. While many taverns served more as socializing and drinking places, Hallsborough Tavern was more specialized, as it served the stagecoach trade and produced more rental revenue than liquor revenue. In its original state, Hallsborough Tavern had no interior staircase, and the upstairs (like that of the Halfway House) could only be accessed via an exterior stair.

William A. Martin was a prominent businessman in the county and was probably the first commercial developer of the Hallsboro area. The great-grandson of a French Huguenot, Martin was postmaster in 1851. After the Civil War, the Martin family continued to run the post office and was joined in the 1870s by William W. Baker, who had married into the family twenty years before. In 1873, Baker and the Martins were engaged in farming, coopering wooden barrels for flour and grinding "shoe make," a colloquial term for the sumac plant. Shoe make was used as a tanning agent, and the tannery at Hallsboro contributed needed capital for postwar reconstruction. Mr. Baker was also active in politics, serving in the Virginia House of Delegates and being instrumental in the formation of the Virginia Department of Health, as well as serving on the Richmond College (now University of Richmond) Board of Trustees.

Retail stores were of vital importance to the economy of the county. Storekeepers lent and "banked" cash and sold most of their goods on credit, with customers paying up their accounts once or twice a year. The storekeeper would sell crops on commission and barter with farmers for fresh produce. Merchants were able to sell liquor; the stores were gathering places in the community, and a store with a tavern nearby would have been an important social center, while also serving as a polling place. The Hallsboro store was about sixteen by thirty-two feet large and probably was originally constructed as a commissary for the large tannery nearby. This store featured a large front room where merchandise was displayed, a back room for storage and a second floor for the living quarters of the shopkeeper. It was most likely built around the turn of the twentieth century. The Martin and Baker families ran the store until about 1928.

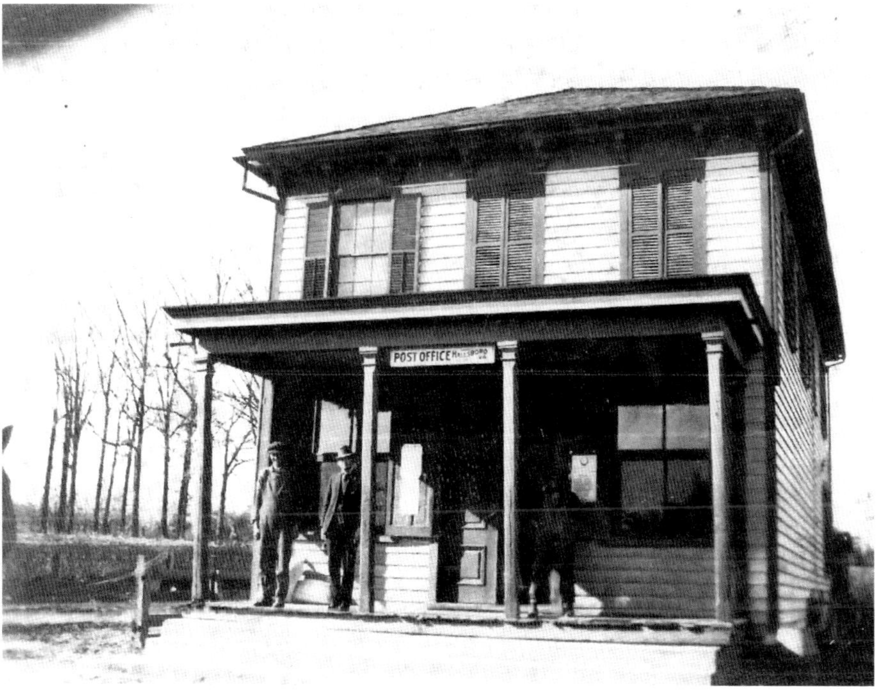

The post office at Hallsboro, circa 1915. *Chesterfield Historical Society of Virginia.*

The post office and depot was first known as Tomahawk. Later, when the post office was moved from the Hallsborough Tavern area to the north a short way, the name was changed to Hallsboro. According to Jeffrey O'Dell's *Chesterfield County: Early Architecture and Historic Sites*, Mrs. Austin Spears, "possibly disenchanted at the removal of the post office from her residence—protested against the duplicate use of the name. Eventually the two parties reached a compromise with the respelling, "Hallsboro." The depot combined a passenger waiting room and freight storage rooms with an uncovered wooden loading platform in front. Both freight and passengers used the depot, which was demolished in the 1950s.

The census of 1850 hints at an interesting human interest story. Caroline Spears, who had married Austin at the age of thirteen, survived her husband and inherited his property. She continued to run the post office and tavern after his death. She rented out land and slaves, administered the plantation and was the legal guardian for her two young children. These were all jobs uncommon for women in those times. Caroline Spears continued to run the estate during the Civil War and managed to hide the family silver in a tree stump during a raid by Union troops at Hallsboro in 1864. Caroline Spears died in 1897.

Privately owned today, and well kept, the Hallsborough Tavern house is a fine remnant of this Chesterfield community. As noted in the application for the National Register of Historic Places, the buildings at Hallsboro are significant because they retain a large amount of their original architectural features and are excellent examples of a late nineteenth-century community in central Virginia. A firsthand and wonderfully personal view of the families and homes of Hallsboro can be found in the Chesterfield Historical Society Library at Castlewood in Ms. Lula Bradshaw Turpin's memoir, written to her cousin, Dick Baker, in 1936, which begins, "In order that you may have a fuller knowledge of your neighborhood, I am writing you in the following pages its history as I remember it."

POCAHONTAS ISLAND

Located across the Appomattox River from historic Petersburg, Virginia, Pocahontas Island is a remnant of an eighteenth-century community with a unique identity. In fact, its geographical legacy is unique in itself. While it was not originally an island at all, but rather was connected by land to Chesterfield County, man-made changes in the topography and the course of the river have created a mystery as to which jurisdiction many of the river areas belong. The usual course of boundary-setting would put a county's boundary in the middle of a river. As the original counties were Charles City and Henrico, it is logical to assume that they set their dividing line in the middle of the Appomattox River. Chesterfield County does not have land records that help to determine which county land masses belong to, and repeated rechanneling of the river through the decades has made old maps ineffective as well. What is known is that in the early 1900s the Army Corps of Engineers created a transportation channel that cut Pocahontas Island off from the rest of Chesterfield.

In 1784, thirty-five years after Chesterfield became an entity separate from Henrico, the villages of Blandford, Petersburg and Pocahontas became united by act of the General Assembly. The newly combined town thrived in its role as an inland port, partly due to the importance of the Pocahontas wharves. Prosperous tobacco warehouses, inspection stations, lumberyards and mills composed this important commercial site. It also became a retreat area from the town of Petersburg as it evolved into a residential community.

Unique Identity

The 1790 census shows 310 free blacks listed in the Petersburg area; by 1860, the number had grown to 3,244. Many of these people moved to Pocahontas Island. "Free Negroes and mulattoes" had to register, and the social system of the time made life difficult for free blacks, whom many whites considered merely "slaves without owners." There were many laws that sought to control their lives, and Pocahontas Island provided a secure place for those who attempted to live outside the mainstream. Although many slaves were freed before the turn of the nineteenth century, free blacks could not vote, serve on juries or testify against whites. After the turn of the century, the free black population exploded in Petersburg and Pocahontas Island due in part to an influx of people of color from Haiti, where white rule was ousted in 1803. These immigrants brought what were considered dangerous ideas with them, to which the whites in Petersburg reacted by forbidding free blacks from carrying guns and requiring them to leave the state within one year of manumission. In 1815, the state relaxed some of these laws by empowering local governments to grant free blacks permanent resident status.

Following the Civil War, Pocahontas Island became home to large numbers of newly freed slaves, something that the economy could not support. Overcrowding and unemployment were rampant. The Freedmen's Bureau helped establish schools, find jobs and arbitrate disputes. This group erected a chapel (the Pocahontas Chapel) for educational, religious and other benevolent purposes. This building stood until the tornado of 1993 destroyed it. A reproduction of the building has since been constructed on the original foundation.

Industry on the Island

Pocahontas Island's recovery from the Civil War was slow. In the 1880s, many residents were employed as carpenters, cooks, merchants, millers, shoemakers and wheelwrights. Increasing industrialization, however, often restricted opportunities for the residents to unskilled labor employment. In the late nineteenth and early twentieth century, coal and ice companies located there, as well as the Columbia Peanut Company, the Pocahontas Distillery Company and the Roper Brothers Lumber Company. The availability of jobs in nearby Hopewell helped increase the population of Pocahontas Island, requiring extra housing.

Famous Residents

Hampton Institute–educated William E. Lee Jr., one of Virginia's earliest black architects, designed the Lee-Dixie House, one of the few two-story dwellings there. Periodic floods swept across the island and drove many inhabitants to "mainland" Petersburg. During the twentieth century, the population declined, and the small stores that were once a focal point of community life in Pocahontas Island were eventually closed.

Citizens, both black and white, worked hard at manual labor on Pocahontas Island. Two success stories were Richard Jarratt and Eliza Gallee. Both were property owners; Jarratt was a successful waterman who also owned his own boat. The Jarratt House is one of the two remaining antebellum buildings still standing on Pocahontas Island.

Relatively little is documented about the lives of the free black women of Pocahontas Island. Eliza Gallee, born free in about 1801, survived an alcoholic and abusive marriage and used a $1,500 inheritance to buy and develop real estate in Petersburg. Interestingly, Gallee herself owned two adolescent slaves.

In one of the island's best-preserved stories, Eliza Gallee mastered a stroke of irony when she purchased the lot of her next-door neighbor in 1857. The neighbor had accused Eliza of stealing cabbages from his garden. She was found guilty and, because she was black, was sentenced to receive thirty-nine lashes on her bare back at the public whipping post. (Had she been white, she would merely have been fined.) Gallee fought back, hiring three lawyers from Petersburg and one from Richmond. Their argument—that Eliza was not black but rather was really a descendant of whites and Indians and, therefore, deserved to be tried in a white court and under white rules—failed to convince the court. Gallee was convicted and sentenced to receive twenty lashes. She took her whipping but most likely got great pleasure in purchasing the property of her accuser three years later.

As a relatively isolated community mostly populated by blacks, Pocahontas Island was likely a stop on the Underground Railroad. Whites avoided the area, many free blacks were involved in fishing and sailing, the railroad ran close by and port and river towns were frequently safe havens for escaping slaves. Sympathetic blacks and river transportation were key to the Underground Railroad, and Pocahontas Island had both. The island still enjoys a strong oral tradition, which also maintains the town's association with the Underground Railroad. One of the original properties is still known as "the Underground Railroad House."

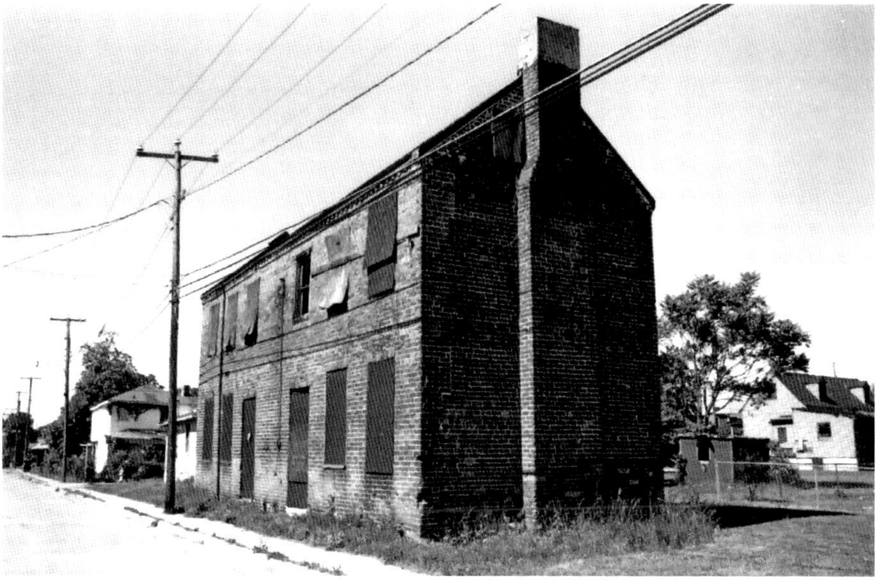

The historic Jarrett House, Pocahontas Island. *Virginia Department of Historic Resources.*

Pocahontas Island Today

On August 6, 1993, a devastating category F4 tornado came to Pocahontas Island. Four people were killed and more than two hundred injured in the Petersburg/Pocahontas area. Many houses on the island were damaged beyond repair, and the beloved Pocahontas Chapel was demolished.

Soon after the tornado, state and federal agencies came to assess damages and evaluate the community's eligibility for listing in the National Register of Historic Places. The team determined that the area was eligible; that determination was followed by the reconstruction of the chapel and the repair and construction of many dwellings. Several sites on the island retain a high degree of physical integrity and have been focal points of archaeological testing to determine the potential for both prehistoric and historic archaeological exploration. Two hundred years of development on the island lends important information about the daily lives and changing fortunes of the island's inhabitants from prehistoric times to the present.

Part IV
HOMES

RAILEY HILL HOUSE: THE STORY OF A HISTORIC HOME

> *For Sale Or Lease for a Term of Years, that well known estate called Railey's Coal Pits, containing 103 acres of land, lying in the county of Chesterfield and state of Virginia, on the Buckingham road and at the termination of the turnpike twelve miles from the city of Richmond. This estate has long been in the occupancy of Major Harry Heth, deceased, and from its great body, and superior quality, has gained a reputation over every other coal mine of the continent.*

Thus read the classified ad from the *Richmond Enquirer* on Tuesday, July 2, 1822, and a prime piece of real estate that was.

Begun only three years after the settling of Jamestown, our county is truly "more than a footnote in history." Chesterfield had the first hospital, the first coal mines, the first ironworks, the first incorporated town, a commercial tramway and commercially grown tobacco. What about the homes and neighborhoods in which our early settlers lived? Railey Hill House, the homestead listed in the ad above, dates back to the 1700s, when the village of Midlothian was a thriving coal mining town. If you can look quickly and closely enough, you can read the iron highway marker on Midlothian Turnpike noting that the Midlothian mines are the oldest in America. Major cities such as New York, Philadelphia and Washington, D.C., imported bituminous coal of "excellent quality" from this small community from about 1730 until the Civil War.

Travel west on Midlothian Turnpike and turn onto North Woolridge Road and then again on behind the childcare center. If you look closely, you can't help but stumble upon Railey Hill House, a small and quaint reminder to those in the know of the way the mine superintendents lived in the eighteenth and nineteenth centuries. County records record Railey Hill House's origins as 1795; author Jeffrey O'Dell records it as circa 1840. All agree, however, that it was built to house the superintendent of the Railey Hill Pits.

In 1810, Martin Railey of Albemarle appointed John Railey to transact coal pit business in Chesterfield County. In 1830, the pits were acquired by the Midlothian Coal Mining Company, and by 1847, these mines formed the largest coal mining company in Virginia. The house was built in two parts, with the second part of the ell being constructed most likely right before the Civil War. The house featured several distinctive architectural details. The main floor doors are unusually large, with heavy Italianate casings. The Federal mantel survived until very recent vandalism in one of the parlors, and at one time a six-foot-high mirror with molded and gilt frame hung over the mantel. This mirror was believed to have been installed when the house was built.

Mining was a difficult life in the eighteenth century, as it remains today. Many mine tragedies were documented in the Midlothian area, and some graves of miners can be found in the Mount Pisgah cemetery. Railey Hill House was an intimate observer to Civil War action, as well, as it became "home" to a contingent of one hundred Federal troops in 1865, following the fall of Richmond. General Philip H. Sheridan dispatched a contingent of troops to that location for the purpose of guarding the mines. The troops camped in the yard for a month or more, and Lieutenant Charles F. Branch, as officer in charge, stayed in the house itself. Local legend has it that Lieutenant Branch made his presence known to occupants of the house well into the twentieth century.

A native of Vermont, Branch enlisted at the age of sixteen. He served bravely and well and recorded in his diary that his regiment entered Richmond on April 3, 1865, on a "beautiful day" and "without opposition." He writes in his diary of visits to the theater and reviews of troops, featuring parades with bands and battle flags. Branch's company was posted in Manchester until it arrived at Midlothian on April 15. Lieutenant Branch made the most of the time he was posted in Midlothian and recorded that he was enjoying his life to an "unlimited extent." Several of the higher ranking mine officers were not native-born to America, and it seems that fact perhaps led them to feel less strongly about the presence of Yankee troops in Midlothian

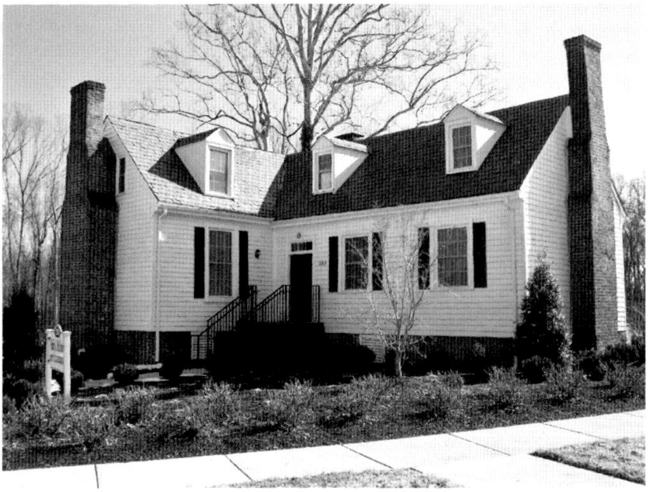

Railey Hill House as it looks today. *Michele Niciphor.*

than native residents would likely have felt. Branch socialized with several prominent families while in residence at Railey Hill and made a special friend of Miss Bettie Jewett, although he had left a girlfriend at home in Vermont, with whom he corresponded regularly. In July of that year, Branch and his battalion left for Norfolk, apparently never to see Miss Jewett again. He didn't marry his Vermont girlfriend, either, but ended up being married three times and having a son and three daughters. Branch died in Vermont, but he left a treasure behind with the etching in the parlor window: "Charles F. Branch, Lt. US Army, address Orwell, Vermont, April, 1865."

Through the years, stories of ghosts have surrounded Railey Hill House, as in many other old historic homes in Chesterfield. Some think that Lieutenant Branch had such an enjoyable stay while quartered there that he returned after his death, while others believe that the ghost is the young son of an early supervisor of the mines. The house is used for offices now, and the casual observer wouldn't guess that there was so much history attached to the modest home surrounded by commercial properties. But there are those who still love the house and have worked hard to see it preserved. As a result of the diligence of the Village of Midlothian Volunteer Coalition, the house has been kept where it is and restored. Although unable to fulfill their dream of moving the house to the site of the Midlothian Mines Park on Woolridge Road, Director Amy Satterfield and her group have worked with the owner/developer of the land under and around Railey Hill House to ensure that the buildings that surround it are architecturally similar to Railey Hill. "If you work hard to make your community a better place to live, it makes life richer for everyone," says Ms. Satterfield. Indeed, the little jewel that is Railey Hill House is a source of delight and enrichment for the community of Midlothian and for Chesterfield County as a whole.

Historic Castlewood: A Witness to History

Imagine the old white house sitting among trees and vast fields in 1775, adjacent to one of the main Revolutionary War supply depots. See it as the home of a county clerk and his family of six children, two of whom died in the house and were buried nearby.

Picture it as a refuge for traveling Methodist ministers in Civil War days. Ponder why the advancing Yankee army passed it by as it drove toward Richmond, letting it stand without damage.

Watch it usher in a new century, undergo "modernization," serve as a bank branch and, finally, become the headquarters and research library of the Chesterfield Historical Society of Virginia.

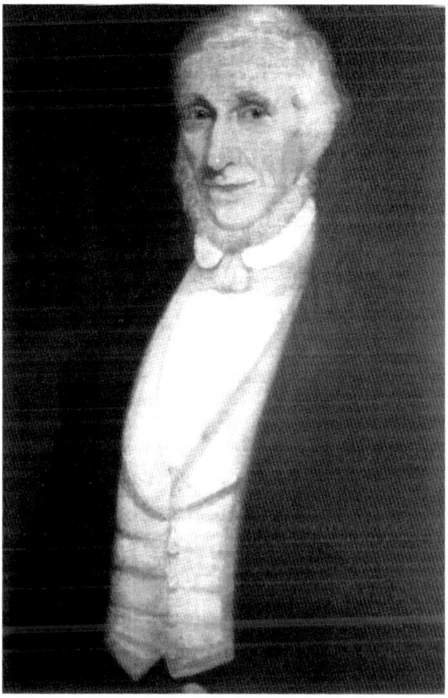

Parke Poindexter, clerk of court from 1812 to 1847 and builder of Castlewood, home of the Chesterfield Historical Society of Virginia. *Chesterfield Historical Society of Virginia.*

The home is called Castlewood, and while many conflicts exist concerning details of its history, it is indisputably one of the historic gems of central Chesterfield. We're so used to traveling Route 10 that we frequently zip by these wonderful old houses, but most area residents are at least peripherally aware of "that old white house that stands back from the road" at the corner of Krause Road and Route 10. What's fun is to stand quietly in the large, tree-bordered backyard, ignoring what goes on out front, and visualize the life that has gone before, leaving mementoes of "trash" buried in the soil.

Architecturally speaking, the house consists of a two-story

gabled main section flanked by slightly different wings. Put together in stages, Castlewood was probably completed in about 1817 and may incorporate parts of an earlier dwelling, as the central segment appears to have stood alone for some time. The wing on the east, known as the ballroom, was likely added next, with the western wing last, although this building is older and was possibly moved from another site. Unusual in this area for its Federal style, Castlewood is one of very few recorded five-part houses. The three main parts were carefully and deliberately brought together into balance; however, the alert observer can tell that the wings are not symmetrical. The Federal style did not gain popularity, as it presented problems of wasted space and lack of communication between the rooms on the upper story. Circulation is poor, and the abundance of wall surface made this style of home expensive to construct.

Castlewood is one of only two early nineteenth-century houses in Chesterfield with a formal room in the basement. The room beneath the parlor is paved with square brick tiles and has a large fireplace trimmed with fine detailing. The elaborately decorative woodwork in the ballroom, along with a fireplace underneath the floor for heating purposes, indicates that the owner was a man of importance and means—someone who entertained frequently.

So, what of the people who built and lived in this house? Parke Poindexter, whose ancestors emigrated about 1657 from the island of Jersey in the English Channel, was born in 1779 and bought the land from William Winfree in 1816. Poindexter had six children, two of whom died at Castlewood in childhood. Upon his death in 1847, his daughter Sarah and her family temporarily lived there following the burning of their family home. The following year, the property passed into other hands until 1860, when it became a parsonage for traveling ministers. Some twelve years later, it went back on the market and was owned by five different families until it came to belong to the William Gilmer family in 1957. Mr. Gilmer was the great-great-great-grandson of Parke Poindexter. The Gilmer family carefully renovated the home and sponsored its designation as a National Historic Landmark in 1976. The following year, it was purchased by Heritage Savings and Loan. This bank, which specialized in "theme" buildings, conscientiously hired experts to research, document and restore Castlewood, and its life as a public building enabled Chesterfield residents to share in its beauty and uniqueness.

Castlewood became a county-owned property in 1992 and was used for various county offices until 1998, when it became the home to the Chesterfield Historical Society of Virginia. The following year, Daniel Mouer, a VCU anthropology professor, led a dig at the site. Mouer found a "robber's trench," the outline left behind when a building is destroyed and only broken bricks

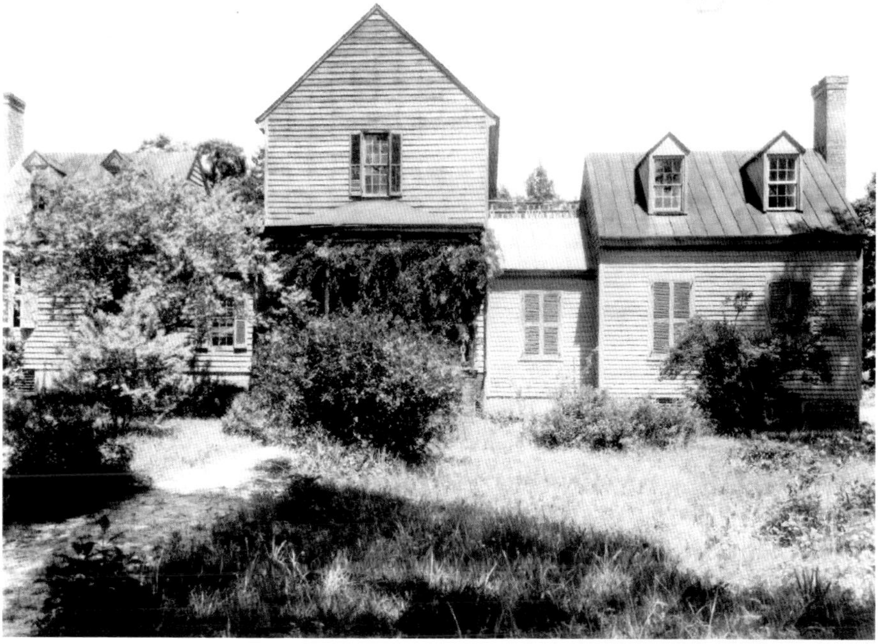

Castlewood, circa 1936. *Chesterfield Historical Society of Virginia.*

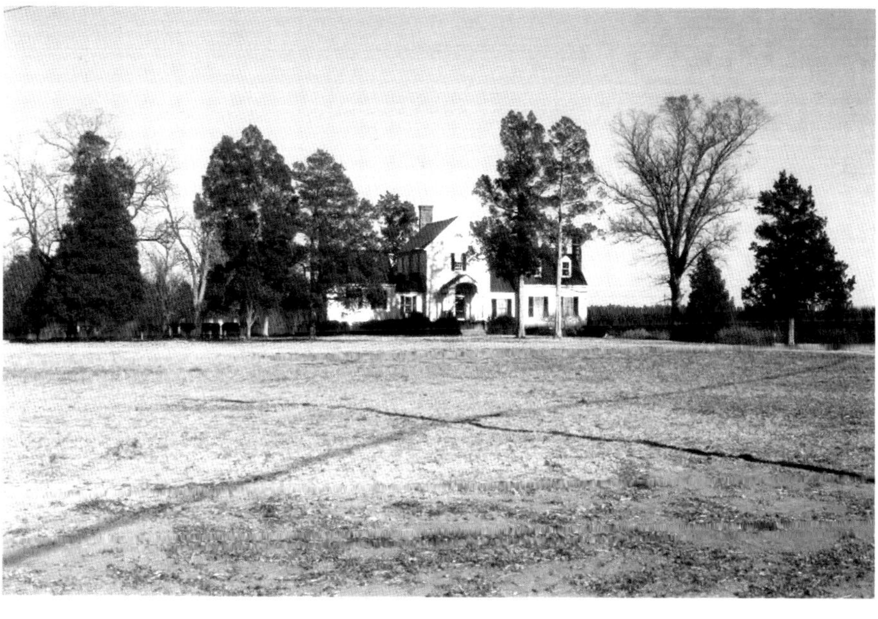

Castlewood in 1968. *Chesterfield Historical Society of Virginia.*

remain. This enabled the crew to discern the footprint of a building in service from about 1770 to 1860 thought to have been the kitchen and slave quarters. Fragments of cooking and personal items were found, along with nails, musket balls, buttons, clay pipes and animal bones—fragments of life long ago, the telltale discards of people long gone.

Sometimes, when one stands in the lush green silence of the backyard, he can imagine the hoof beats of horses galloping to the supply depot nearby, looking for munitions, clothing or food for Patriot forces. Or maybe they belong to the army of the Confederacy as it moved just slightly east to the Battles of Yellow House, Chester Station and Drewry's Bluff. A microcosm of colonial society, the fragments of plantation life can still be found in the soil of this property: the cooking devices of the slaves in the kitchen, the toys of the children, the buttons and jewelry of the women and the bullets, bones and shells that were the trash of generations long gone.

Have you looked at it lately, as you've driven down Iron Bridge Road? Has the glint of the sun off the new metal roof, handcrafted by restoration artisans, drawn your attention? Have you wondered, "What is that building?" Come on in and look for yourself. Come hear the whispers from the past.

The Chesterfield Poorhouse

Nestled within the boundaries of Pocahontas State Park lies the site of Chesterfield's former poorhouse or almshouse. Built to house the elderly and destitute before the 1930s establishment of the Social Security system, the Chesterfield poorhouse served this purpose for one hundred years. Closed in 1924, the poorhouse has gone the way of many other landmarks replaced in 1936 by the park, such as the tracks of the Bright Hope Railroad and the Fendley water station, along with many family home sites. Old maps, aerial photos and plats of the park, as well as the Pocahontas Park master plan research, have identified the area beside a logging road southwest of Woodpecker Road and northwest of Mount Gilead Methodist Church as the likely location of this complex. The story begins in the year 1755.

Hening's Statutes at Large (the collection of all the laws of Virginia, from 1619 to 1792) of May 1755 charges Virginia church vestries with "the lodging, maintaining, and employing of all such poor people as shall be upon the parish." In October 1810, a court order was recorded in Chesterfield that a group of men was to fix on a proper site and make a plan of the necessary buildings and related expense to erect these buildings, to be reported back to the court. In the September court of 1811, the report was made and the group of men assigned this task were further appointed commissioners and ordered to purchase the land and make necessary repairs to existing buildings or erect others, for the reception and accommodation of the poor. In November 1811, Thomas Burfoot Sr. sold to these commissioners a tract containing one hundred acres, "more or less," and the building was begun. The very first occupant of the poorhouse may have been Absalom Traylor, born in 1791 and listed as being there in December 1811.

A 1922 plat of the poorhouse property shows 97.2 acres and five buildings. A group of Chesterfield Historical Society of Virginia members researching the poorhouse several years ago spoke with a longtime Chesterfield resident who remembered visiting her grandmother, the cook at the poorhouse, in the early twentieth century. She recalled one large house and other outbuildings. The remains of a brick foundation have been found, which may have been the larger building or perhaps the overseer's or superintendent's house. Census reports showed the overseer as head of household, and his family members and the occupants of the poorhouse are listed together. Sources indicated that the buildings were torn down in the 1960s.

It is likely that there was a cemetery at the poorhouse. Documents show money paid for digging graves and making coffins, and there are death certificates listing burials. Several years ago, a site near the complex was located with spring flowers and roses, such as often remain from early graveyards. There were no marked graves, but some fieldstones were located in the area—a primitive and cost-free way of denoting a burial space. Expense records for 1853 show money paid to G.W. Mahores for making a coffin, digging a grave and burying Mr. Edwin Powel on April 1, 1853, for five dollars. Elizabeth Burton was paid for digging a grave and furnishing a shroud on the same day. A 1912 death certificate was found for Richard Cheatham, who was between "70 and 80 years" and was buried at "Chesterfield Poorhouse." In 1918, John Lifton's death certificate listed him as an "old man," born in Hungary and buried in the "Co. Alms House."

We don't know what the conditions were like at the poorhouse. Records of purchases of staples were the same as what could be found in most homes: bacon, flour, sugar and corn. Inventories show common household items such as bedding, clothing and shoes. Vegetables like potatoes, snaps, turnips, squash, cabbage and corn were grown. Medicine, tobacco and whiskey were bought. Even forty-six gallons of brandy were made and sold. Doctors' bills were paid, and fabric was purchased for the making of clothes. Fees were paid for the nursing care of occupants and for the cost of a carpenter's work. A typical listing of expenses from the year 1853 showed the following items:

- *1 coffee mill, 75 cents*
- *39 2/4 yds osnabarge* [sic], *$3.45*
- *1 hhd bacon, $64.71*
- *Flower* [sic], *sugar, $13.38*
- *Mary Godsey and blind children, $22.50*
- *2 pare* [sic] *scissors, $.31*
- *Dr. William Weisiger's medical bill, $20.00*
- *Philimon H. Wilkinson for 25 bbls corn, $87.50*
- *For board and nursing, John Shadrock, Irish boy while sick, $3.00*

Conditions at the poorhouse seemed dismal by 1889 when a commissioner instructed to investigate reports on the management and condition of affairs presented his findings. Nine "inmates" were housed there at the time of the report: Sam Wells possessed only "one pair of second-hand pants. Bed and bedding furniture by himself," and his "physical condition is of such a character as to render the room and bedding unbearable by the stench and odor"; Nelson Fowler was "an old inmate…scarce of clothing…no winter clothing whatsoever"; Mary Andrews had "no bed clothing…and a calico dress"; and Nathan Cary was "tolerably well supplied with clothing and bedding…bedstead entirely worthless."

The inhabitants of the poorhouse varied greatly. Most were white and ranged in age from infants to the elderly. Other than paupers, there were the "old and infirm," blind, disabled, orphans and women and their "bastard" children, as well as probably those who just had no other place to go. Many lists still exist giving names and dates of birth and/or death, and these can be found in the auditor of public accounts records, overseers of the poor reports, federal census lists, death certificates and death register entries. Many of these sources are in the form of loose records. Most are incomplete and have not been published in any form. These records can be tracked down in the Library of Virginia and the Local History room at the Chesterfield Central Library, as well as the Chesterfield Historical Society of Virginia library at Castlewood.

Our county has changed a great deal in its four-hundred-year history, and many similar stories exist only in library records and in the memories of longtime Chesterfield residents. The Chesterfield Historical Society of Virginia is especially interested in the recollections of our senior citizens and encourages them to share their stories with friends and family so that they can be preserved.

Part V
BUSINESSES

QUARRIES AND MILLS: CHESTERFIELD'S EARLY INDUSTRIES

England's King James I established the London Company of Virginia to launch colonies in the New World. The company sold stock to finance its operations, and part of the sales technique was promoting stock purchases as a show of patriotism. The London Company also touted the numerous opportunities for settlers in the New World, only to be forced to deal with the diminishing colony at Jamestown. Due to high mortality, Jamestown was not proving to be a profitable endeavor, and soon the settlement at Henricus felt the pressure to produce. The London Company pushed for the establishment of towns and industry, but Virginia started out as a rural community and stayed that way for generations; nonetheless, it experienced steady economic growth due to the abundance of natural resources, diligent leadership and people who were motivated to succeed. Tobacco, once it began to flourish, was a quick cash crop at the Bermuda Hundred end of what was then the county of Henrico. In 1701, coal was found, and that industry began on the opposite end of the county. The south-central area had the ironworks at Falling Creek, and granite quarries and clay mines sprang up on the northern edge. Henrico/Chesterfield was becoming a self-sustaining community. Unfortunately for the London Company, none of this happened in time to return stockholders' investments.

Quarries

The northern part of Chesterfield was home to granite quarries as early as the 1830s. It was expedient that granite was found on the banks of the James River, making for ease of transportation. Railroads crossed over the granite banks, and with the development of industry following the Civil War, Chesterfield's granite became known and appreciated by people from other parts of our country.

There were several quarries strung along the tracks of the Danville (Southern) Railroad in the area of the Powhite Creek. One of the more interesting small quarries was located at the lake in Forest Hill Park, where it is fed by Reedy Creek. Holden Rhodes, owner of the quarry, built the only Richmond-area stone house, which he named Boscobel, in 1843 from his quarry's stone; the house still stands today. Other quarries were Westham, McIntosh, Krimm, Middendorf, Hawkins, Old State, Old Dominion, Netherwood, McGranigan, Donald, James River, Wray, Old Netherwood and Rhodes. Netherwood Quarry produced stone used in paving, churches, homes and monuments.

In the 1870s, huge orders for granite were transported to the Manchester area for cutting into workable blocks that were then shipped by barge to

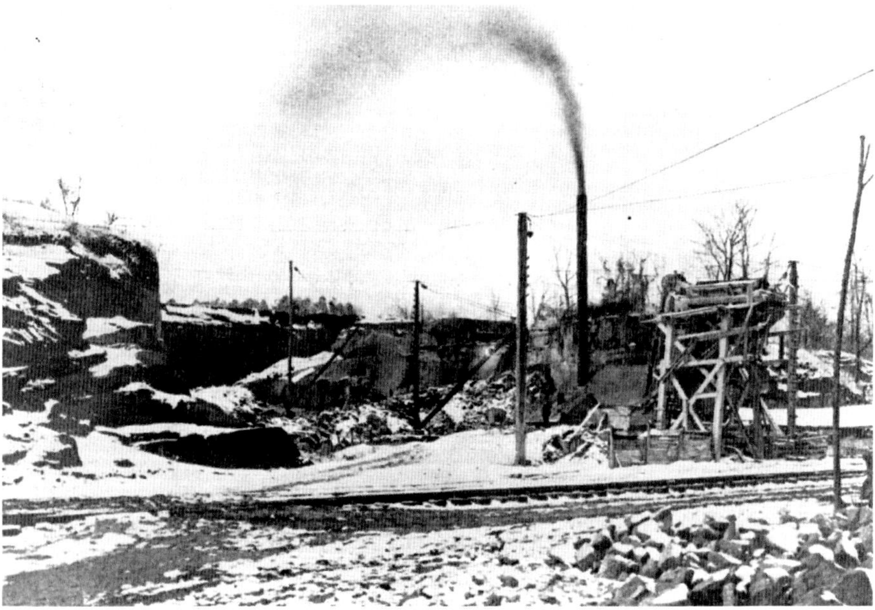

The Netherwood Granite Quarry near the James River. *Chesterfield Historical Society of Virginia.*

Washington, D.C., for use in the construction of the State, War and Navy Department buildings. Our own Richmond City Hall and main post office featured Chesterfield granite, and the stone for the steps and wings of the state capitol addition came from the McIntosh Quarry, which was the largest in the state by 1911. Chesterfield's granite can be seen today in the Soldiers and Sailors monument on Libby Hill and in the All Saints Episcopal Church and was transported as far north as New York City.

Chesterfield granite was shipped to St. Louis and used in the piers of the huge Eads Bridge stretching across the Mississippi River. In 1877, prospective purchasers from Ohio came to Chesterfield to inspect the stone with the intent of purchasing it for street paving, as was common throughout the North.

Even in the nineteenth century, the government involved itself in the regulation of this industry by establishing a U.S. Laboratory staffed with federal agents to inspect and test the stone. Stonecutters were white men in the 1800s, while black men did the labor. Many of the stonecutters were brought in from the North and were able to make sufficient money to purchase land and settle in the area. The companies also built barracks to house the workers; some squatted on vacant land, and others commuted via the railroad. Many quarry workers were former slaves who gradually acquired their own land and formed a community on Old Bon Air Road. The Westover Hills area, annexed from Chesterfield in the 1970s, still recognizes an area called Granite, which was delineated by the railroad tracks that turn northwest at Powhite Creek. Several quarries were located in this area, which had a railroad station called Granite; a village and post office grew up around it. A black settlement was also part of this area.

"The granite industry flourished for about the span of a man's life," reported the *Virginia Cavalcade* magazine in 1954, "and quietly died with the age of asphalt, concrete and steel."

Mills

Settlers coming to a new land needed to attend to many things quickly. Food and shelter were top priorities and could be readily provided in crude or raw forms. It wouldn't be long, however, before the need arose for a mill to be built within the boundaries of a community, and Chesterfield County had many. The *LaPrade Map of 1888* shows some thirty mill sites in the county at that time.

Early American mills were called grist-, corn or flour mills, and they served the vital function of turning grain into flour or meal. Farmers would bring their own grain, and the miller would process it, charging a small price called a "miller's toll." Mills were water powered, with a water wheel that turned gears connected to a drive shaft; having multiple gears enabled the shaft to turn more quickly than the water wheel turned and to grind the grain faster. Some mills had two stones, and the distance they were set apart from each other determined the fineness of the finished grain. Some mills had threshing and cleaning facilities so that the farmer could bring his raw grain straight from the field, and others dealt only with "clean" grain.

Sawmills were often built in conjunction with gristmills. The first sawmill was built in 1610 by Captains Edward Brewster and George Yeardley, who built a fort and mill below the falls of the Appomattox. Wood finished by this mill was floated downstream to Jamestown, to be used in the building of the fort palisades and homes in that colony. By 1611, the London Company was sending mechanics from Europe to build mills and get the building of homes started in the New World. By 1632, there were several sawmills operating in Henrico/Chesterfield. Because of its geography, with its two major rivers and two significant streams, Falling Creek and Swift Creek, Chesterfield was perfect for the industry of milling. By the late 1800s, the steam engine had led to the development of portable steam-powered sawmills, and water was no longer used to power the mills.

When tobacco yield began to decline in the 1760s, wheat became a dominant crop, ushering in the era of different types of mills. Most gristmills were built by a local planter to serve his own needs and, perhaps, the needs of his neighboring farms. He might charge a toll of 15–20 percent for his services. Merchant mills were large mills that produced refined white flour as opposed to the whole grain flour produced by the private mills, and these were often built by wealthy farmers and, later, by groups of investors. Commercial mills bought the grain directly from the farmer and dealt in large quantities that might be sold domestically and abroad. This exporting of flour required locating these commercial mills near shipping ports, where the flour could be readily loaded and shipped to Europe, the West Indies or South America. Naturally, the merchant and commercial mills were larger than the private mills, having multiple wheels in operation and being two to four stories in height and made of brick and stone, while the private mills were smaller and simpler.

The government also had a presence in the mill industry, and mills were regulated by the General Assembly. If a man owned land on one side of a stream that he wanted to use as his mill, he had to petition the General Assembly and pay a fee to have the opposite side classified "condemned." As early as 1667, the General Assembly passed the Mill Acts, which provided for the passage of boats through locks on large streams. The General Assembly also fixed the rates that a miller could charge for grinding corn and wheat.

William Byrd I owned a large milling operation on Falling Creek in the late seventeenth century and was looking for markets abroad. By 1711, William Byrd III ran a tannery and sawmill in the same place, called Ampthill Mills after the property of Archibald Cary, which it adjoined. Although the mill was destroyed and rebuilt about 1800, there remained a mill in that location that processed corn and flour until the early years of the twentieth century.

Murchies Mill was south of Pocoshock Creek above the confluence with Falling Creek, in the approximate vicinity of a gunpowder mill during the Revolutionary War. It is believed that this mill was built by Cary and destroyed by Benedict Arnold's troops, who dumped the powder in the creek. This was the first powder mill in America.

Brander's Mill, on Swift Creek, was owned by John Brander. A Scotsman who came to America shortly before the Revolutionary War, he recognized the natural water power resource and the future that it promised for the milling industry. This mill was located near the present-day Pocahontas Park where Branders Bridge Road crosses Swift Creek, and it turned out meal and flour in such abundance that, with its neighbor, Rowlett's Mill, the General Assembly ordered a new inspection station to be built there to serve the two mills. A small village surrounded Brander's Mill, including a house for the miller and a bakery.

Gregory's Mill was located on Falling Creek near Rockwood Park. It was a gristmill, processing flour and meal; at one time it had an adjoining sawmill. R.B. Winfree originally built a mill in this spot in the 1850s, before selling to James Gregory, owner of nearby Rockwood Plantation. The mill functioned until 1950, producing barley, rye and cornmeal. Sadly, the picturesque old mill was destroyed by arson in 1987.

Swift Creek Mill stands on the spot of its several predecessors. It was built in the 1850s as a grist- and flour mill. The Swift Creek Manufacturing Company purchased it in 1852, and the office of the present-day theater was probably its company office. Henry Randolph I was known to have built a mill around this spot in the mid-seventeenth century that his descendants operated until 1804. The mill is noted in insurance records as being a merchant mill, corn mill and sawmill. During the Civil War, battles raged all around Swift Creek Mill as Confederate general George Pickett tried to hold Union general B.F. Butler's troops from their march to Richmond. The mill transitioned into a distillery later and passed through several owners, continuing in operation until 1956. Used as a popular live theater today, it is the oldest mill in Chesterfield.

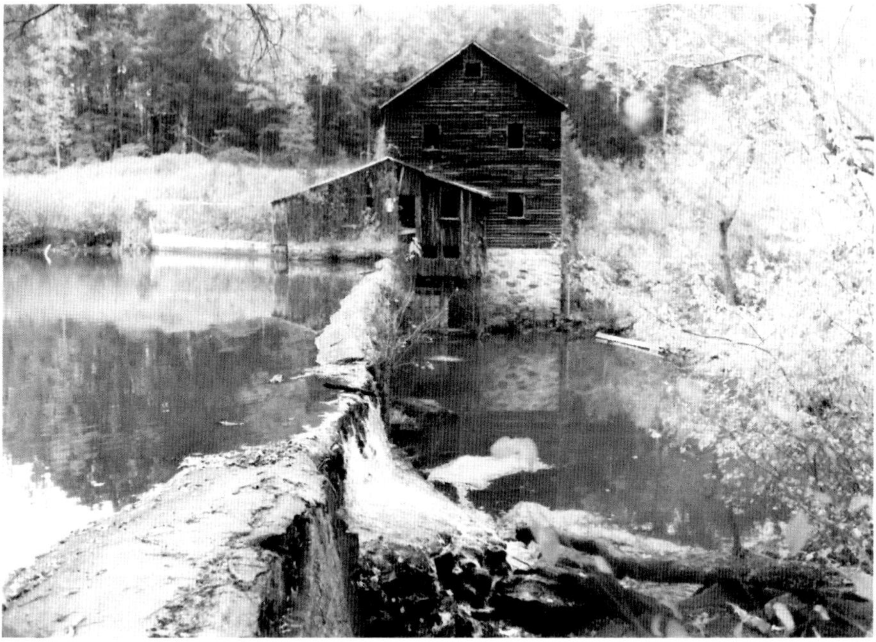

Gregory's Mill, taken in 1983 before it was destroyed by fire. *Chesterfield Historical Society of Virginia.*

By 1621, the London Company was in severe financial trouble, and the Indian massacre of 1622 put its existence in dire straits. As the Crown proposed several measures that restricted the company's authority in governing the colony, stockholders rejected them. King James soon changed the status of Virginia, making it a royal colony to be administered by a Crown-appointed governor in 1624. The London Company did not last long enough to appreciate the fruits of its labors in the New World.

Bottled Water: An Old Industry in Chesterfield County

One doesn't need the wisdom of the ages; by midlife, most of us realize that it's true that there's nothing new under the sun. Centuries ago, right here in Chesterfield, people were murdering one another, families underwent tragedies, young women had babies out of wedlock and wayward children were still taking their toll on their parents. And then there's bottled water. Nothing new there, either.

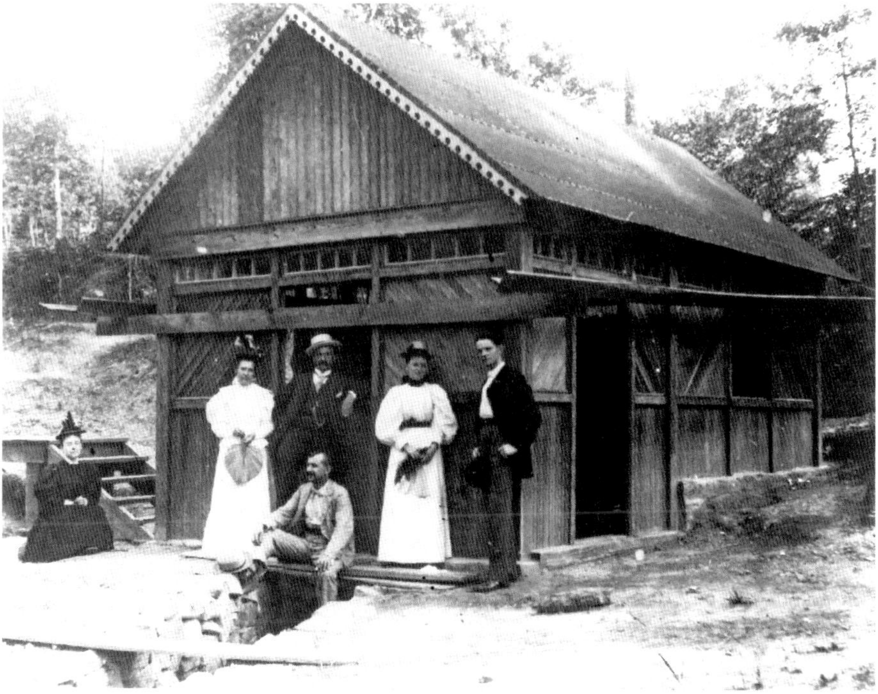

Jahnke family members at Beaufont Springs, built by the Beaufont Lithia Springs Company, which bottled water for daily use in Chesterfield kitchens, photo circa 1896. *Chesterfield Historical Society of Virginia.*

Venture to today's northeastern edge of Chesterfield, where not so long ago the "something new" was Cloverleaf Mall. Many of us can cast our minds back thirty-odd years to when there wasn't much out that way, but even further back that area was known as Beaufont Springs. This area was originally called Crow Spring and was later renamed Beaufont (French for "beautiful spring") by its purchaser, James Robertson, when he bought it in 1895.

Robertson developed it commercially the following year and called his company the Beaufont Lithia Springs Company. Why Lithia? If you look the word up, you find that it is a derivative of the Greek word "lithos," meaning "stone." From the stones of granite at Beaufont came water that was promoted as having special therapeutic properties.

The Beaufont Lithia Springs Company bottled water for use in drinking and cooking and was very popular with Richmond-area residents. The interior of the springhouse still shows where the water used to flow. In 1817, a Swedish student named Johan Arvedson discovered lithium, but it is widely believed

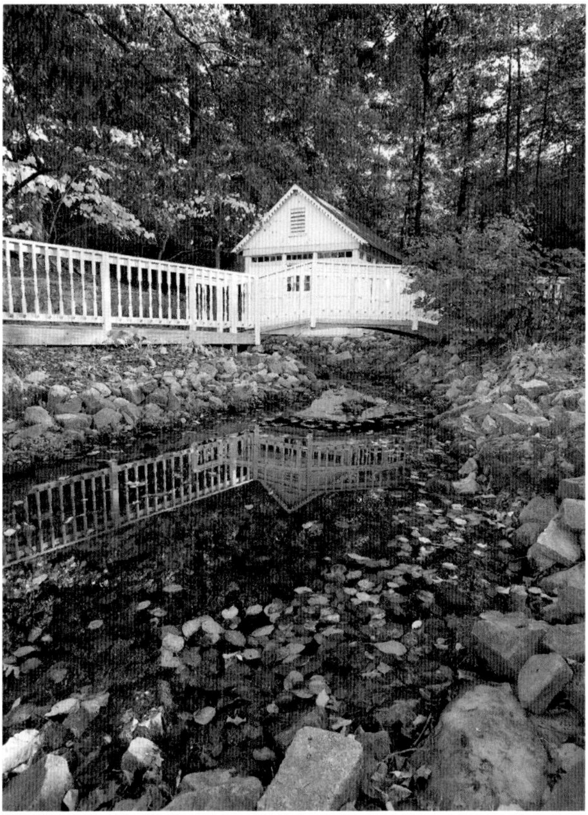

The Beaufont springhouse at the present time. *Page Dowdy.*

to have been in use for ages, possibly in southern Egypt before the birth of Jesus Christ. In the late 1800s, the Lithia Springs Sanitarium was established in Georgia. It used natural lithium water in treating alcoholism, opium addiction and compulsive behavior. Manic depression had not been identified as a mental illness at that time. Lithia water was analyzed and found to be rich in lithium, potassium, calcium, magnesium, fluoride and other essential trace minerals.

Back at Beaufont, Robertson and his son were taking their spring water downtown by horse team. From there it was shipped to cities such as Washington, D.C., Philadelphia and New York. The company changed hands in 1916, and business boomed during prohibition. The new owner, Frederick Sitterding Sr., added six to eight flavors of carbonated beverage to his inventory. These "soft drinks" led to the formation of a sister company, Climax Beverages.

Sitterding owned another company called the Home Brewery, which joined forces with Beaufont Springs, adding a brewery and ice plant to the joint venture, which lasted until 1933. By then, municipal water systems had improved to the point that bottled water was not in such demand, and the water-bottling part of the business was shut down in 1940.

The area of Beaufont Springs enjoyed a brief revival in the 1950s when the Sitterding family built a picnic ground and recreation area around the spring. This area was available for rent and for business parties and was quite popular. Volleyball, basketball, horseshoes and a dance pavilion were well-used amenities. Caterers were used to bring in food, but renters were required to purchase their beer and soft drinks through the company.

Upon construction of Chippenham Parkway and the commercial properties in Beaufont and the Boulders office park, the water became muddy, but the springhouse bottling plant and picnic area were preserved by Sigma Development, the developers of the Boulders. According to earlier newspaper reports, these areas can still be visited today.

In 1999, the medical profession celebrated the fiftieth anniversary of the discovery of lithium, a miracle drug that truly changed the way mental illness is treated. But mankind was aware of the spring's healing qualities well before then.

Chesterfield's Mining Story

Between the years of 1610, when Sir Thomas Dale first ventured up the James River to the area that is now Chesterfield, and 1626, when it was dissolved by order of the court, the London Company was under great pressure to make the colonies bring money into English coffers. The company was always a "for profit" undertaking, and the nearly ten thousand immigrants sent to America by means of the company were expected to produce goods to that end.

Colonists soon found that there was no gold sitting on top of the land and no gems floating in the streams. Using the abundant natural resources, they experimented with tar production, wine and beer making, glassmaking, silkworm cultivation and timber harvesting, but in the early days colonists were so busy trying to survive in this new land that they had little time to develop new industries—ones that could often be developed more cheaply at home in England.

John Rolfe discovered that tobacco flourished in Virginia's soil and that the cultivation of this plant was a boon to the colonists. Not only did it enhance trade with England, it did so with the Indians as well. The discovery of coal in 1701, however, was the impetus that changed numerous aspects of life in Chesterfield County for many of its populace for almost two centuries.

Chesterfield's Coal Mines

Chesterfield is part of a large basin called the Richmond Coal Basin, which runs from western Henrico and eastern Goochland south to the James, with portions of Powhatan and Amelia Counties included. It is estimated that in the early 1800s there were 1.5 billion tons of coal in this basin. Closest to the surface in western Henrico and in Chesterfield, the coal basin is disc shaped and dips four thousand feet at its deepest point. The total length is 33.0 miles, and it is 9.5 miles at the widest point; the total area is 190.0 square miles. The size of the individual coal beds ranged from five to forty feet, with the thickest beds in Midlothian, where the biggest part of the coal basin lies.

It was the French Huguenots, religious refugees given land on the James by King William of England, who first discovered coal in the northwestern part of Chesterfield in 1701. The second area of coal discovery was the Midlothian village area, in the mid-1700s. Legend has it that a slave in the early 1800s found coal just lying on top of the ground in Winterpock. The coal was of good quality, but its potential was not immediately realized. Robert Beverley in his *History and Present State of Virginia*, published in 1705, wrote that wood was easier to get and had more uses: "And as for Coals, it is not likely they shold [*sic*] ever be used there in any thing, but Forges and great Towns, if ever they happen to have any; for, in their Country Plantations, the Wood grows at every Man's Door so fast."

Coal began to be commercially mined in the 1730s, but only about three tons of coal was mined in the period from 1780 to 1840, most of it for domestic use. Indeed, it took a while, and a war, for the potential of coal to peak. By the time of the Revolution, England had put such a high tariff on imported coal that there was renewed impetus to the commercial mining operation. As people were moving away from heating with wood at about this time, coal saw an increase in demand. Mining sources geared up, and by the end of the Revolutionary War, Chesterfield coal was being shipped to the northern colonies. Thomas Jefferson in his *Notes on Virginia* declared the coal produced in Chesterfield to be of excellent quality, and he used Midlothian coal in the White House.

The *American Journal of Science and Arts*, in April 1842, reported, "It appears that the Mid Lothian coal of Virginia is substantially the same as the best coals of both Europe and America, while it is almost identical with the Newcastle coal of England," and called it an excellent fuel for a parlor grate.

Chesterfield historian Bettie Woodson Weaver, in the *Virginia Cavalcade* 11 (Winter, 1961–62), wrote that Chesterfield coal was the only significant source of coal in the entire Confederacy and that it fueled the furnaces at Tredegar Iron Works, which supplied soldiers with nails, wheels, cannons, shells and other items necessary to fight a war; this was one of the reasons that the capital of the Confederacy was moved from Montgomery, Alabama, to Richmond in 1861. After the war ended, the Yankees hastily secured the mine property and tried to keep some of the now-freed black men around to work them. A detachment of Union soldiers was housed in the historic Railey Hill House, former home of a mine supervisor in Midlothian, where Lieutenant Charles F. Branch of Orwell, Vermont, etched his name in a window pane in April 1865.

Mining Process

Shafts began to be sunk in the mid-1700s to mine the coal; before that, shallow trenches were hand-dug, and when a coal deposit was located, the trench followed the deposit. After shafts allowed mining to go below ground, coal was raised from the mines in crates called cowes. These crates held about two bushels of coal each and were raised using mules. The cowes were also used to pull water up out of the mines. Mining mules were used down inside the mines as well and were even stabled below ground. Mines operated twenty-four hours a day, and workers had twelve-hour shifts. Mines did not operate on Sundays.

Mining was inherently a risky business, and foreign experts were brought in to consult on safety issues, as well as technique. Many miners were asphyxiated by poison gas or coal dust, and many died in explosions. Mining presented an attractive career option for many young English and Scottish engineers and experienced miners, who were attracted by the possibility of becoming landowners in the New World.

A significant portion of the miners were enslaved and were leased out by their owners. Some were free blacks. Coal mining in Virginia dwindled after the Civil War as the composition of the workforce changed. Additionally, by the late 1800s, Appalachian mines were producing a better quality of coal, and their technology had advanced beyond that of war-stunted Virginia. Mining became too costly and the coal seams too irregular to follow; many of the formerly prominent mines were abandoned. During the Depression, people were allowed to go in them and help themselves to the coal.

Impact of Coal Mining

In addition to its inherent value for producing heat, coal "sparked" progress in the area of transportation in Chesterfield. Old Buckingham Road, the precursor to Midlothian Turnpike, was paved in 1803, making it the first paved road in Virginia. The paving was necessitated by the damage done to the dirt-surfaced road by teams of four to six horses hauling millions of bushels of coal from the mines to the river. In the summer, the dust was choking, and in wet weather the road became rutted and impassable. The Manchester Turnpike Company charged a toll to transport coal to Richmond, and its profits were used to keep the road in decent shape. The company asked the legislature for permission to levy higher tolls on coal wagons, and so much coal was moved along this road that its stockholders earned a dividend on their investment.

Still, profit-seeking mine owners sought a faster way to move greater quantities of coal, and two coal pit owners named Nicholas Mills and Beverley Randolph obtained a charter from the legislature to organize the Chesterfield Rail Road Company in 1828 to cover the thirteen miles between their mines and the James River below the falls. With no government assistance, $100,000 worth of stock was sold, and an engineer named Moncure Robinson was hired to supervise the construction.

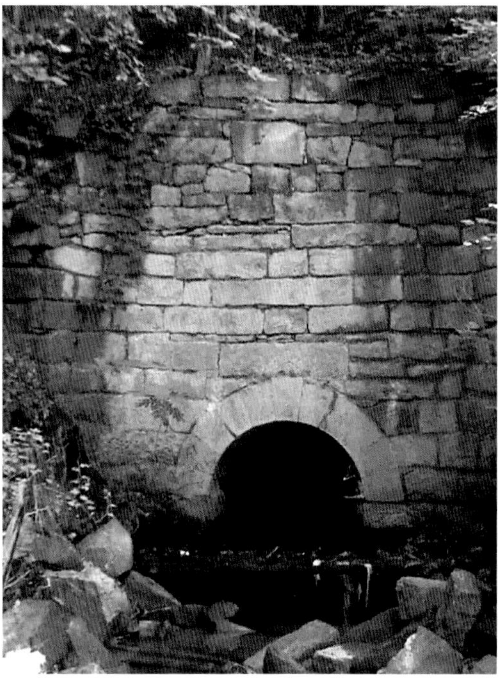

A remnant of the historic Chesterfield Railroad, this railroad arch dates back to the mid-1800s. *Mike Likins.*

Taking advantage of the natural incline of the terrain, Robinson built a single-track tramway of wooden rails overlaid with scrap iron. Gravity moved the cars from Manchester to the river, as it did at the upper end of the route. In the middle of the route, horses and mules assisted in the process. Remarkably, the device that turned the cars at the top of the line operated by turning cables attached to both ascending and descending cars around a large drum. As the drum turned, it wound two cars up while two went down. Cars were manufactured by inmates at the Virginia State Penitentiary.

Taking shrewd advantage of the launching of this new transportation route, and seeking to add to the coffers in order to continue developing the line, Mills invited his friends on a trip in the "pleasure car," a boxcar-type container with rough plank seats pulled by mules. A couple dozen businessmen traveled uphill to the mines, where they were fêted at a barbecue. The tramway remained in operation for twenty years and made Mills rich. He was reported to have $800,000 in gold in the bank when he died in 1862.

After serving the coalfields for many years, this primitive form of transportation progressed to a whole network of steam-driven railroads, many lines of which were laid on the region's canal towpaths, and that became the predominant means of transporting coal.

Names of Mines

The *American Journal of Science* in 1841 lists some Midlothian mines as Cunliffes, Blunt's, Gowrie Pits, Black Heath, Raileys, Sallee's, Trabue's and Wooldridge's. The Black Heath mines were owned by the Heth family and were located near the present-day Robious Crossing. Rich with coal, this area was initially mined in the late 1780s but was abandoned because of the danger and expense of getting the coal out. Scotch miners were brought in by Heth, and three shafts were dug. A steam engine was used to pump out water. Black Heath was also the name of the Heth mansion, birthplace of Confederate general Henry Heth on December 16, 1825.

Southwest of Black Heath lay Thomas Blunt's mines, which Blunt leased to Heth and later to the (A)Etna Mining Company. Blunt employed ninety miners, most of whom were slaves. During his first year in operation, a fire caused flames that shot two hundred feet above ground. Etna exhibited its coal at the World's Industrial and Cotton Exposition in New Orleans in 1884.

The Wooldridge family's pits were located in the present-day village of Midlothian area and included the Grove Shaft, centerpiece of today's Midlothian Mines Park. These pits employed 150 men and boys and twenty-five mules and produced hundreds of thousands of coal in a good year. Wooldridge also had a steam engine to lift the coal and water out of the pits, as well as a hospital, doctors and a church for his black workers. This church

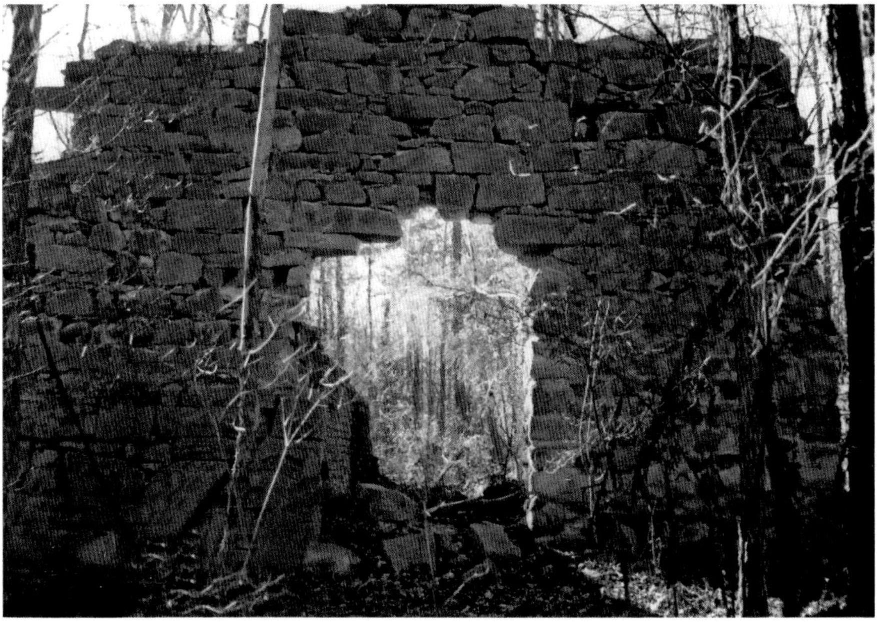

The Grove Shaft Mine, photo taken in the early 1990s. *Chesterfield Historical Society of Virginia.*

is the oldest African American church in Chesterfield County, established in 1846, and is now known as First Baptist, Midlothian.

Abraham Wooldridge, Dr. Archibald Wooldridge and others established the Midlothian Coal Mining Company, which became the largest and most successful mining conglomerate in the area. The company continually made capital improvements, and in their first five years of operation the pits produced 1 million bushels of coal each year. The Grove Shaft was the last operating mine in the Midlothian area, closing in the 1920s.

Mining Disasters

A visit to the old Mount Pisgah church cemetery tells another, more human side of the mining story. It has graves of several men killed in the mining disaster of March 1855. This tragedy was preceded by an explosion in 1850 at the Raccoon Pit in Clover Hill, which took six lives; another in the same pit six years later claimed seventeen, followed by a third in 1859 with the loss of nine men.

The *Daily Dispatch* of April 6, 1867, reported on the catastrophe at the Clover Hill pits, where an explosion "has proven to be one of the most awful calamities with which this country has ever been visited, carrying into eternity in an instant, in a manner sickening to the mind by its merest contemplation, 69 souls." The writer hastened to clarify:

> *Now, it is a fact that the presence of inflammable gas in our coal veins is not a general feature of the coalfield. Sections only of the field are infected with this terrible enemy…not one shaft in fifty…has discovered the existence of one cubic foot of inflammable gas. Therefore, as terrible as this accident is, it should not prejudice operations in our coalfield, which is gradually working itself into the confidence of shrewd investors and we trust will, as it should before many years, become a great source of wealth to our city and our State.*

The fact was that "damps," or buildups of hazardous gasses, were inescapable elements of coal mines, and mining was a dangerous activity. Aside from health threats and the risk of collapse, early mines had constant ventilation challenges, suffocation, flooding issues and firedamp explosions (caused by sparks produced by metal striking pyrite-laden coal), which caused larger coal dust explosions that could quickly engulf an entire coal pit. The *Daily Dispatch* of February 4, 1882, reported on the explosion at the Grove Shaft that took thirty-two lives. "It is now believed beyond doubt that the thirty-two men who were in the pit are all dead. It is supposed they were instantly killed by explosion. If any survived it, they were suffocated by carbonic acid gas soon afterwards," the paper reported. Workers in that mine averaged $1.50 a day and were tasked with one hundred bushels a day, which would take eight to nine hours.

Although a comprehensive record of mining accidents does not exist, the *Virginia Division of Mineral Resources*, published by the Department of Mines, Minerals and Energy in 1988, lists thirty-one accidents between 1810 and 1912.

The Mines Today

As late as the 1920s, the then flooded Grove Shaft mine was drained, reinforced and worked by the Murphy Coal Company for a few years before becoming cost-prohibitive. The Gulf and Shell Oil Companies completed studies of the old mining areas in the 1970s to determine the feasibility of piping out methane (natural) gas, if it was found, and to consider mining the residual coal. Little of that work remains, although there are still tons of coal beneath Chesterfield's surface. A walk in the Midlothian woods, in the few areas that have not been developed, can lead to the unexpected discovery even today of indentations that could well be the top of a leaf-filled mine shaft.

Though no longer a pillar of Chesterfield's economy, the influence of the coal mining industry is an integral part of our history. In 1870, one of the first acts of the county's first board of supervisors was to commission a county seal with the dominant depiction of a coal miner leaning on his pick beside the flowing water of the James.

A Visit to the Old Country Store

Imagine a place where you could swap a dozen eggs for some sugar and sell your excess tobacco crop while you were there. You could purchase your necessities and pay at the end of the year, borrow money until the crop came in, buy licensed liquor and collect your mail. You could sit around a potbellied stove, smoking your pipe, sipping spirits and talking politics in the dreary winter months. All of these were the norm in Chesterfield's old general or country stores.

The neighborhood mercantile was an important part of life in Chesterfield in the eighteenth and nineteenth centuries. After trade with Britain largely disappeared following the Revolution, necessary supplies were obtained by wealthy plantation owners, who could order in quantity and store goods on their land for resale to their neighbors. Called plantation stores, these were the forerunners of the country or general store, and a pretty competitive situation existed between them. Large plantations were really self-contained villages, and they had skilled workmen or slaves who could make tools, wool, wooden furniture and leather goods, the surpluses of which could be sold to smaller neighbors. People didn't have the disposable income we are used to, and their demands were small. Peddlers were common as well, bringing necessities to the doorstep and eliminating the need to travel very far.

In 1936, Frank Beard's Grocery Store in Chester was located on the ground floor of the Eyler Building. Dances, plays and other entertainment were held regularly on the second floor. As transportation, wealth and trade in general increased in the 1800s, country stores began functioning. The industrial revolution made goods available more cheaply and widely. People had more money to spend, and plantation stores ceased functioning as retail outlets. Jeffrey O'Dell in his book *Chesterfield County: Early Architecture and Historic Sites* tells how the country storekeeper lent and stored cash, sold on credit, functioned as a crop commission agent and bartered goods for

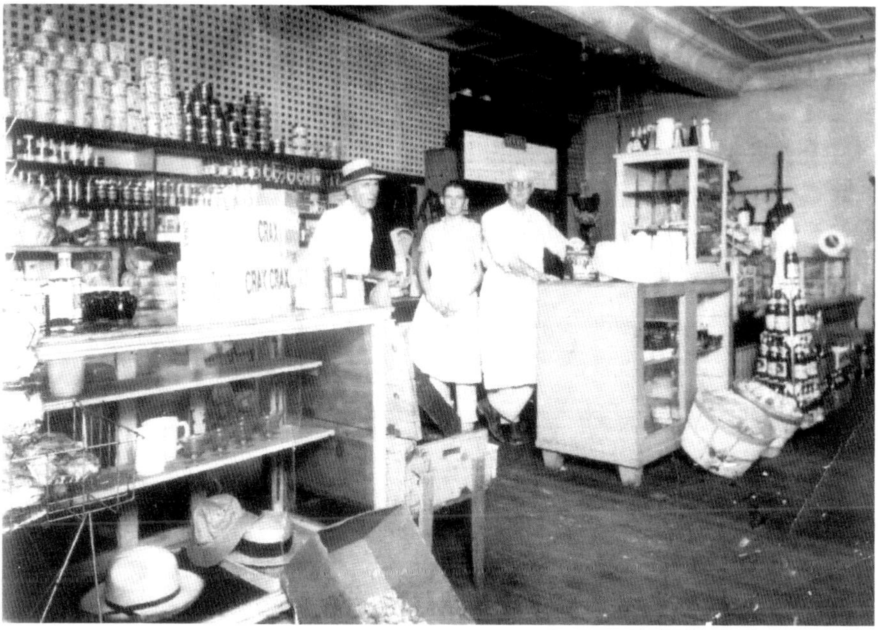

Frank Beard's Grocery Store, Chester, 1936. *Chesterfield Historical Society of Virginia.*

farmers' produce. Country or general stores took on a central function of life in a community as they became gathering places for social entertainment, post offices, polling places, transportation hubs and, sometimes, taverns.

In 1853, Frederick Law Olmsted wrote about a store located near Petersburg (possibly in Chesterfield), saying that it was "a little cabin, which fronted… upon a broad and well-traveled road. Over the door of the cabin was a sign, done in black, upon a hogshead stave, showing that it was a 'grocery,' which, in Virginia, means the same thing as in Ireland…a 'dram-shop.'" He continued, describing a room flanked with shelves containing all manners of old and new goods, a table, a fireplace, a bed and a spinning wheel.

O'Dell's book reports that licensing fees were required of Virginia storekeepers, and by the tax records we can tell how many stores operated during a time period. Between the 1820s and 1850s, Chesterfield had about forty general stores; most were located in the western part of the county, farthest from the trading centers of Richmond and Petersburg. In the 1840 census, the average value of Chesterfield store buildings and merchandise was $787.50 per store. Since this is well below the state average, it hints that most farm families in Chesterfield did their shopping in one of those cities.

Agricultural improvements in the mid-1800s, along with the emancipation of slaves, brought more wealth and more consumers to the county, and the number of stores increased along with the standard of living for the average Chesterfield resident. Entrepreneurial northerners and former farmers liberated from the land became interested in setting up shop in Chesterfield, and the availability of better shipping means made goods more easily obtainable. The heyday, reports O'Dell, of the general or country store in Chesterfield was from the 1870s to the 1920s. After that, the widespread use of the automobile ushered in the era of going to the city centers to shop, and country stores were pretty much just that—the small building down the road in the boondocks that carried just the basic necessities of rural living.

Structurally, general stores were pretty much alike. Most were about twice as deep as they were wide, with a front porch, a large front room for displaying merchandise and a smaller backroom for the owner's office. Seed, fertilizer and agricultural items might be held in a lean-to or exterior shed. The inside walls were lined with shelves, and windows were regular sized and often secured by bars or shutters. Counters ringed the wall, and larger stores might have had two aisles, display tables and hanging racks. Lunch counters were often located in the back, and foodstuffs in bulk were found in barrels. In the larger or wealthier stores, display cases might be found. The large iron stove was always located in the center of the room, with lots of seating around it. Some stores were shared by fraternal organizations whose lodges would be upstairs.

O'Dell found twenty pre-1920 rural stores in Chesterfield. Only one was brick; the rest were frame. They ranged in size from sixteen by thirty-two feet to twenty by forty feet. The owners usually lived in a part of the structure, and often gas stations were also a part of the enterprise. Some stores stood by a major road, while others were part of one of the villages that made up Chesterfield, like Ettrick, Matoaca and Midlothian. These stores were generally bigger and more elaborate, carrying more specialized items. Alpheus Horner's store, built in 1910, occupied one room of his huge Victorian farmhouse. This store, which served the public as well as Horner's sawmill employees, can still be seen at the Victorian Square shopping center on Hull Street Road.

A far cry from the shopping world of the twenty-first century, country stores in Chesterfield demonstrated a simpler life, when one's credit was his good name, when shopping actually was "one stop," when customer service was truly personal and when the country or general store was the center of community life.

Part VI
The Way They Lived

Mincemeat Illegal in Chesterfield County and Other Assorted Christmas Customs

Although they don't remember the illegality of mincemeat, longtime residents of Chester Helen Patrick, Jane Dean and Patsy Murphy recently reminisced about other local Christmas traditions, many of which are things of the past. Strolling down the memory lane of the Depression era, they recalled the harbinger of Christmas: the tree at the old post office. Girl Scouts and the local Lions would decorate the tree, and "then you knew it was Christmas," said Patrick.

Here in Chesterfield, the population in 1900 was only 18,800, and communities were widely spread out within the mostly rural and agricultural county. Churches served as the central gathering or social centers within a community and were the natural location of Christmas celebrations and pageants. Homes were decorated in addition to churches, but not as much entertaining was done in individual homes. Mrs. Patrick remembered the churches still being the focal point of social activities and celebrations throughout the year in the first third of the twentieth century. Her father ran the store on the corner of Ecoff Road and Route 10, and Patrick remembered the excitement at Christmastime when the store windows were decorated. Christmas caroling at homes of shut-ins, her father decorating the tree on Christmas Eve (it had to be cedar) and oyster stew on Christmas morning were favorite memories for Jane Dean. Gifts were not the focal point of the season, she asserted. Although gifts were traded within the family, a child might get one gift, and that might be something that he or she needed, like shoes or a dress. Other special goodies were fruits like oranges, apples and grapes, along with nuts.

Sledding on Ferguson Hill or on the Curtis Street hill and ice skating on the pond down there during Depression years were favored activities, when no one knew what they didn't have for Christmas, because their friends and neighbors didn't have it, either. Patrick remembered her first bicycle, paid for with the earnings from her brothers' newspaper routes. "I still carry on traditions that mother had in our family," said Mrs. Dean. She continues to make candy for nieces and nephews, as well as special calendars of fabric and glitter.

Lifelong Chesterfield resident Jerry Rudd grew up on a poultry farm off Bliley Road in the area that was annexed to Richmond in the 1970s. He remembered a childhood in the World War II era, when "you just didn't expect much." His mother baked fruitcakes after the war; during the war, it was hard to find ingredients due to rationing. Rudd remembered a Christmas when he was ten or eleven when he really, really wanted a BB gun. His father traveled with the power company and found a secondhand gun in Norfolk, which he bought and refinished. Young Jerry awoke at about 3:00 a.m. Christmas morning and found the gun under the tree, still tacky: "I think mama told me it had gotten too close to the candy." Rudd's father or uncle would go hunting and shoot a goose or turkey for Christmas dinner, and their tree always came from the woods around their farm, which at that time was undeveloped country.

You might not think of Virginia as a liberal state, but back in colonial days it was considered rather liberal in the celebration of Christmas. Believe it or not, the making of mincemeat pie was regarded as a sign of excess and was banned by the Puritans in New England. Feasts are certainly a key element of holiday celebrations today, and even back in the 1700s mincemeat was an important traditional dish down South. In fact, colonists in Virginia went to rather great lengths to create this delicacy, as the fruit, cinnamon and nutmeg had to be imported.

Williamsburg today portrays a beautiful illustration of a colonial Christmas that embellishes a bit on reality. For the early colonists who settled in Williamsburg, Christmas was a holy time. Settlers were predominantly English, so their holiday celebrations reflected English traditions. Christmas wasn't really a time for children; it was a time for church, feasting, dancing, fox hunts and visiting friends and neighbors. Gift giving, when it was done, was done from superiors down and was not reciprocated. That is, parents might give a child a book or some sweets, and their servants would get some remembrance, but they were not gifted in return by those parties.

The way that a home was decorated told a lot about the owners, and people used what was at hand—namely greens such as holly, bayberry and boxwood from the woods and garden. To add color to greenery, fruits were added, and the pomegranate in particular was an indication of affluence. Seashells, pine cones, pineapples and apples (which were not native to Virginia then) also garnished the greenery. There might be a yule log, usually of oak, which was considered to bring good luck to the house. Traditional food selection was limited. Fresh fruit, as mentioned, as well as vegetables, were a luxury, as preservation was not possible. Meats, however, were slaughtered in wintertime and were in plentiful supply. Depending on the wealth of the family, alcohol was abundant and was often given as a Christmas gift from owners to their slaves.

In colonial days, the Christmas season began on December 25 and lasted until January 6. New Years was not celebrated, and the song "The Twelve Days of Christmas" was thought to be a gimmick to teach children to count and not really holiday-related.

During the short era known as the Federal period (1780–1820), the season remained confined to the twelve-day period between December 25 and January 6, but it involved a more elaborate style of socializing. Grand banquets were presented, with pyramids of fresh fruit and dozens of desserts. The height of the social year, many couples chose to be married during this time, George Washington and Thomas Jefferson, with spouses, among them.

In the years before the Civil War, traditions in the South flourished. The symmetry and discipline represented by the Federal style of architecture carried over to seasonal decorations, which were restrained and elegant. *Grandiose* was desirable, and again evergreens dominated. Ivy wreaths and garlands were popular in woodwork, and fresh flowers began to be used to decorate for special occasions. Forced bulbs and potted plants were commonly seen. Although grand in scale, in quantity, less was considered better.

The years between 1840 and 1900 brought in the Victorian era, and excess was the keyword. As states in the North continued to pronounce celebrating Christmas sinful—declaring the reading of the Book of Common Prayer, the making of mince pies, the playing of cards or any other Christmas celebration illegal—in the South it was an important season, with the partying and dancing beginning in some plantations at breakfast and continuing until afternoon, and it was the southern states that first declared Christmas a legal holiday. After the Civil War, the growing availability of children's books and women's magazines helped spread Christmas customs around America.

It was during this time that Christmas trees and poinsettias were first reported. Originating in Germany under Prince Albert, ornately decorated tabletop trees had branches set wide enough apart to safely light candles and so that large gifts, ornaments and edible goodies could be hung on them. In Virginia, the cedar tree was popular, but its delicate branches made the use of lighter ornaments necessary. The tree was decorated by the older children and/or adults. It was often kept locked away and lit by the father on Christmas Eve or Day. As late as 1900, only one family in five had a tree; they were more often seen at church or school than in homes. The first description of a floor-to-ceiling tree was at the end of the 1800s. In 1902, President Teddy Roosevelt had a room at the White House decorated for visiting royalty. Looking like a fairyland, it was decorated with garlands and lavish flowers and was reported on by many newspapers and magazines of the period.

Father Christmas became St. Nick in the Victorian period, changing from a pioneer-type figure to the jolly elf dressed in red and fur. Gifts were given to everyone: kids, servants, friends and strangers. Caroling became popular. Children and adults spent lots of time making decorations for home and church, using popcorn, cranberries, holly berries and leaves.

Other than in Sunday school and elementary school, most modern-day tree decorators don't make their own Christmas decorations anymore. Our fond holiday memories of the later twentieth century are more likely to be mall-oriented in some fashion. Many Chesterfield residents, including central-Chesterfieldian Jean Collier, remember trips to downtown Richmond to see the windows at Miller & Rhoads Department Store. Collier's memories of the late 1960s and 1970s include the new Cloverleaf Mall and taking her son to see Santa there. Her favorite Christmas memory is of the first Nativity scene that she and her husband purchased, at Standard Drug Company for one dollar. "Although I've been given many Nativity scenes since, that one is still with me and will always be my favorite," Collier declared.

Christmas has changed through the ages—some may argue not wholly for the better. Throughout, however, some things remain constant. Christmas is a time for faith and the decorations and celebrations of church, for family and the quiet and special times spent with loved ones, for celebrating the things that lift us out of the everyday and the things that bring joy, build memories and establish traditions.

Chesterfield School Board Minutes, 1941: A Glimpse into Our Past

Franklin Roosevelt was in his third term as president, Charles Lindbergh was testifying to Congress in support of a U.S. neutrality pact with Hitler and Winston Churchill was appealing to the U.S. populace to send arms to Britain. Cheerios breakfast cereal was introduced, and *Citizen Kane* premiered in New York City. Carving on Mount Rushmore was completed, and Pearl Harbor was bombed. The year was 1941.

School Board Meets

At regular intervals that year, as now, the Chesterfield County School Board met to discuss matters of importance to the citizens and taxpayers of the county. Board members, men with names we have come to know like Cogbill, Chalkley and Wells, met to conduct board business at the 1917 courthouse on Iron Bridge Road. Minutes from prior meetings were reviewed, and new business was opened for discussion and consideration. Review of the minutes of the school board, available on microfilm in the Local History room of Central Library, gives us a peek into the not-so-distant past, as well as introduces us to people and places that are no longer part of our county.

A list of the schools' names shows some that we all recognize today, as well as some that are found only in old-timers' memories and in the annals of documents: Chester, Grange Hall, Manchester, Matoaca, Summer Hill, Hickory Hill, Beulah, Centralia, Good Hope, Gravel Hill, Kingsland, Midlothian, Mount Nebo, Ochre, Piney Branch, Pleasant View, Port Walthall, Midlothian High, Bellemeade, Bon Air, Broad Rock, Colonial Heights, Ettrick, Enon, Union Branch, Union Grove, Warwick Road and Winterpock.

By the Numbers

The county school payroll in 1941 was $24,159.85. Additional expenses were incurred when substitute teachers had to be called in, and the pay varied between assignments. Mrs. Michael Cifelli substituted two days at Chester and was paid $7.00, while Mrs. Lucille Transou made $16.00 for four days. A day at Ettrick brought Mrs. Charles Carater $3.50, and Mrs. R.L. Johnson was on duty for four days at Hickory Hill for only $8.50.

In each board meeting, expenses and receipts were enumerated. Fred Thompson reimbursed the county in April 1941 for $3.55 worth of "telephone tolls," and the Commonwealth of Virginia issued a gas tax refund of $5.60. Typically, the expense report was much longer than the income report and reveals some prices we wish we could see today. The gas, oil and supplies for Mr. Cummin's bus amounted to $22.81 that April. Telephone service for Midlothian High was $5.30. Water service at Bellemeade School was only $2.00, and fourteen tons of slack coal for Chester was a whopping $70.00. Warwick Road School needed wood costing $13.50 for three cords, and Mr. H. Elmer Myers supplied ten cords for Centralia and Piney Branch. Midlothian, Manchester, Hickory Hill and Gravel Hill were supplied with twenty tons of coal for heating, at a cost of $47.95.

The Stories

Enlightening and nostalgic as these accounting notes are, the human interest stories and everyday life vignettes are even more so. January 1941, a month that brought the U.S. ambassador to Japan's report of rumors of a surprise attack on Pearl Harbor, in Chesterfield brought a request for approval of the rental of classrooms to Chester Methodist Church for Sunday school use at the rate of fifty dollars. The board also voted that January to approve sending the superintendent to a conference in Atlantic City that cost the taxpayers seventy-five dollars. The Works Progress Administration presented a request through the superintendent to use one classroom in "the Matoaca School" for special classes in adult education. Classes were to be held afternoon and evening. "Since it was learned that the WPA did have another place they could use, and due to the fact that it would be necessary for this Board to keep the building warm at nights and furnish janitorial service, it was ordered… that the request be denied," the minutes record. The January meeting also dealt with a bus driver who had failed the drivers' test twice and was ordered to either "furnish a competent driver for his bus or relinquish his contract with the School Board."

The superintendent was asked by the board to draw up a salary schedule using as a basis for teachers' salaries a minimum of $650 per session and a maximum of $1,200, except for "special" teachers (undefined) and principals.

A special meeting was held on January 29, 1941, to make a decision for the new high school building at Chester. A contract was awarded to the English Construction Company of Altavista for $99,700. This bid was lowered from the original $120,850 by exclusions or cost-cutting measures such as leaving the stage in the music room unfinished, omitting the PA system and using cinderblock instead of glazed finish

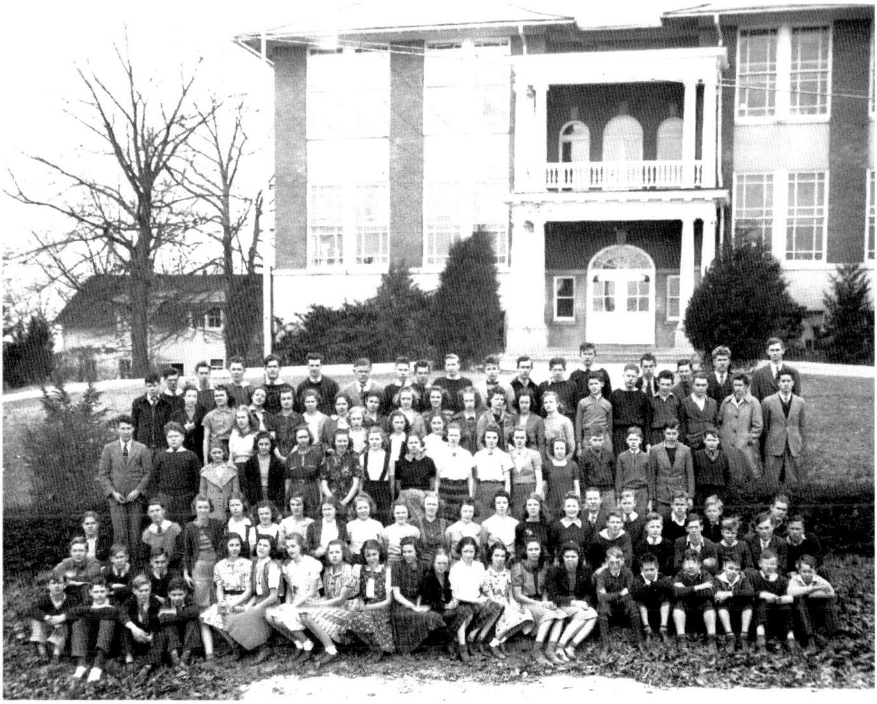

Chester High School, circa 1942. This building became Chester Middle School upon the completion of Thomas Dale High School. *Chesterfield Historical Society of Virginia.*

on the side walls of the gym. Substituting A grade yellow pine for birch saved $723 on the inside trim, and using plaster instead of acoustical tile in the corridors trimmed the budget by $600. By the request of the judge of the circuit court, the board voted to begin preparing for a bond issue referendum to raise $200,000 for the construction of Chester and Manchester High Schools.

Equal Rights

Also in January, a delegation of representative patrons of Good Hope, Pleasant View, Winterpock and Beulah Schools presented a petition asking that the board consider the transportation of students from their respective communities who had completed seventh grade to Hickory Hill High School and that a bus be provided for this purpose in the annual budget. The board voted to have a committee appointed to consider this proposal and report back at a following meeting.

In March 1941, the National Gallery of Art in Washington, D.C., was opened, and the Grand Coulee Dam began generating electricity. In Chesterfield, Oliver W. Hill, attorney representing the Chesterfield County Branch of the National Association for the Advancement of Colored People (NAACP), and a delegation of black citizens of the county appeared before the board urging an answer to the petition they had presented the previous December in which citizens and taxpayers of Chesterfield and the county branch of the NAACP requested that the board take action to equalize the black teachers' salaries with the white teachers' salaries.

The board had provided a $100 salary increase to each black teacher in its 1941–42 school budget. "Upon consideration whereof and on motion of F.G. Laine, it is resolved that it is the policy of this Board to adopt a single salary schedule for all teachers, effective beginning with the school session 1942–43." And on the topic of salaries, a special covenant inserted in teacher contracts for all teachers for school year 1941–42 decreed that "said teacher or party of the second part agrees that the amount of salary may be decreased for inefficiency or increased for outstanding work during the session on recommendation of the Superintendent, provided that no salary may be decreased below the minimum of the adopted schedule."

In May, Bob Hope performed his first USO show, and here at home, Mr. Redd, the superintendent of Bethany Home, an orphanage on Forest Hill Avenue, requested that the high school pupils living there be sent to Manchester High School instead of Midlothian and that the elementary students to go to Broad Rock instead of Bon Air. This request was denied.

Hot Topics

In July, Joe DiMaggio's fifty-six-game hitting streak ended, and Chesterfield's school board minutes show instructions to advertise the old shop building at Chester for sale and to sell it at public auction to the highest bidder. In a matter eerily similar to recent issues, the matter of discontinuing high school at Grange Hall and transporting the pupils to Manchester was presented at the July 29 meeting. This decision on the part of the school board was challenged, and school board member H.L. Gill began the August 6 meeting with a request that the board rescind the proposal. "He further stated that the people in that community were exceedingly anxious to have the school reopen next session," the minutes read. His request was fully discussed by the board, after which Mr. Gill presented the following: "Be it resolved that the Board rescind its former motion taken at an adjourned meeting held at the Courthouse on July 29 by which the high school department at Grange Hall school was ordered closed as of next session, and that the school be reopened for next session and that a principal and the necessary teachers be employed to operate the school as before." The motion did not receive a second. Fellow board member F.G. Laine moved that the former action of the school board with reference to the closing of the high school department at Grange Hall be sustained and that the high school department at that school be discontinued. This motion passed.

The school closure issue continued at the next meeting of August 21, where it appears that a "committee representing a large delegation of citizens from Clover Hill District conferred with the Board, again requesting it to reconsider its action of Tuesday, July 29, at which time it was ordered that the high school department of Grange Hall be discontinued and the pupils transported to Manchester. Various members of the delegation, Mr. H.L. Chalkley, Member of the Board of Supervisors from Clover Hill district, Mr. J.G. Hening, member of the Board of Supervisors from Dale, and Mr. H.L. Gill, Trustee from Clover Hill District, spoke in favor of continuing the school. Mr. Gill once again moved to rescind the former Board action. This time, the motion was passed with five ayes and one nay."

Following this climactic issue, a following entry concerns the approval of a request for the purchase of a new school bus for $800 "for Levi Johnson's bus route."

Fall school board meetings brought discussions of changes to bus routes, bus driver salaries, special permission for students to enter kindergarten before age six and an intriguing statement that "this Board will not be responsible and will not take any part in the educational program at the CCC [Civilian Conservation Corps] camp located at Beach, VA until the present Educational Supervisor there is removed and a suitable director has been placed at that Camp." The induction of the principal of Beulah School, J. Wilson Crump, into the military service prompted the school board to send a resolution requesting his deferment citing the dearth of teachers and "especially those qualified for principalships."

Progress and Change

Of great interest to county residents was the resolution presented that fall concerning the completion of the changeover from Chester High to a school with a new and historically important name:

> *Whereas Sir Thomas Dale, Lt Governor of Virginia, under the Royal Charter was the first man to organize a definite settlement in Chesterfield in which a few years later in 1619 the University of Henricopolis on Henrico Island and a public school on the site of the present Coxendale Farm, were established and Whereas this effort toward establishing a school system in the New World was the first made by English speaking people, and whereas it appears desirable to give a historic name to the new high school at Chester, Now, therefore, be it resolved that the name of the present Chester High School be changed to Thomas Dale High School of Chesterfield County, Virginia.*

As our nation inexorably moved toward war, the end of the year brought new salary considerations, with a pay schedule that "shall apply to teachers in Chesterfield County for the session 1942–3 and for subsequent sessions until this schedule is changed or revised by the School Board." The scale ran from $700 to $1,300, with consideration based on preparation, experience, efficiency, intellectual ability, personality, background, the teaching duties assigned and quality of service rendered, general fitness or teacher-like qualities and supply and demand. It was noted that pay above the maximum could be allowed by the school board on recommendation of the superintendent due to graduate work, extra service on the curriculum or research work or assignment of other additional duties. The minutes go on to read, "The salary of any teacher may be reduced or increased during the school session upon recommendation of the Superintendant and approval of the School Board when it appears that the classification of the teachers should be changed due to inefficiency or to outstanding work."

The year 1942 would bring challenges anew to Americans and to Chesterfield residents. Annexation issues began to creep into the minutes of the January 1942 school board meetings, with the implications for the schools that would be affected, including Richmond taking on shares of debts and management of schools. The division superintendent was authorized to purchase a car to be used exclusively for school purposes, with said car to be kept at the courthouse and to be "one of three makes, Ford, Plymouth or Chevrolet." A committee was formed to work out some type of adjustment to the superintendent's salary if and when said car was furnished. Challenges, conflicts, adjustments and compromises—this look into the issues of yesteryear brings both nostalgia and a fresh perspective to those that we face in Chesterfield today.

Equines and Equestrians

As far back as the thirteenth century in England, horse racing was documented as a popular sport, and the early American colonists brought their love of horses with them to the New World. In addition to their use in transportation and farming, the racing of horses provided entertainment for their owners by appealing to man's basic interest in gambling and winning. Chesterfield played an important role in the history of horse racing in America, with both two- and four-legged residents figuring prominently.

Horse racing in early America was equal in popularity to cockfighting, cards and dancing. Well-bred racehorses were brought here from Great Britain on a regular basis. Even common farmers took pride in the horses they managed to breed and own, and fine horses were a sign of status in the community.

In Virginia, horse racing began under the tenure of Governor William Berkeley, who had a plantation called Greenspring located near Jamestown during his terms of office from 1641 to 1652 and from 1660 to 1677. The state capital at that time was Williamsburg, and that city had a fine horse track that boasted races each spring and fall. The oldest racetracks in the Chesterfield area were at Petersburg and in Richmond proper, but Chesterfield also had a track on present-day Broad Rock Road. Early racetracks were straight; circular tracks where more people could observe the action came later on.

Henrico County court records from 1670, when Chesterfield was still part of that county, record disputes over races. The owning, breeding and racing of fine horses was a passion shared by prominent citizens such as Chesterfieldian Thomas Jefferson, grandfather of our third president.

Horse racing largely left the central Virginia area after the Revolutionary War, partly because owners of fine Virginia horses had sent them to North Carolina to keep them out of the hands of raiding Tories. Following the war, the toll taken on the land, as well as ex-soldiers who were coming home to face large debts, precluded the luxury of continuing to devote time to the raising of horses. Horse racing went to the Roanoke River area, where the land was better suited. Warrenton, an area that remains focused on horses even today, featured a top-notch school for boys, the Warrenton Academy. The presence there of well heeled boys whose fathers visited them regularly might have served to further the area's popularity with racing enthusiasts. Another factor that put a damper on horse racing throughout Virginia was the anti-betting legislation enacted after the Revolution. This development forced the business of horse racing, along with the profits it reaped, to Maryland, Tennessee and Kentucky.

In Warrenton, a prominent breeder and trainer of horses was being raised. Tobacco farmer and Warren County clerk Marmaduke Johnson was an avid horse racer, and his son, William Ransom Johnson, was brought up among fine stables and well-to-do young men who were accomplished in hunting and shooting. Many had served in the war and were competitive and restless. They enjoyed betting in sports like cockfighting and horse racing. Young Johnson learned well and brought his skills to Chesterfield when he married Mary (Polly) Evans, daughter of a Revolutionary War physician who was given land in Chesterfield after the war and who was also a racing enthusiast. Johnson lived in Chesterfield until his death in 1849.

Meanwhile, Chesterfield resident Thomas Goode (1745–1813) had already been breeding horses on his plantation off Ivey Mill Road. He was the son of John Goode, III, and Marjory Branch Goode of Chesterfield. He married Agnes Osborne in 1769 and served as a justice of the county court in addition to sheriff. Goode bought horses when they were finished racing, and his acquisitions included Shark, a British horse born in 1771 and considered "the Champion of the Turf" in England. Goode's ambition was to breed Shark to become the preeminent sire in Virginia, but another England-born horse called Diomed (1777) would overtake Shark's reputation.

Interestingly, Diomed was originally brought to America against the advice of his new owners' agent. He was twenty-one years old and considered a bad stud. In those days, studs were moved from farm to farm, and Diomed worked actively, siring Sir Archy (Archie), the greatest champion of his day, and Lexington, born in Kentucky and considered the greatest stallion of his time.

Johnson purchased Sir Archy when the horse was recovering from distemper and not racing well. He paid $1,500, took him home to Chesterfield and coddled him for a season until he recovered. Johnson, a short, handsome man with flowing gray hair and striking features, was considered to be fearless. It was said that Johnson had only to look at a horse to determine how well it could run, and he owned enough of the best racing horses to be called "Napoleon of the Turf." The complete list of horses Johnson owned is not known, but he owned dozens of them and trained many more. Consulted for advice by horse lovers such as Henry Clay and John Randolph, Johnson's plantation, called Oakland, adjoined Eppington, and it was recounted that Johnson, Clay, Randolph and other prominent citizens of the time enjoyed sitting on the plantation's front porch and watching the horses run on the track in front of the house.

Johnson produced more than twenty champions and won sixty of sixty-two races in the 1806–7 racing season. One of his purses was $30,000. But horse racing was not all that Johnson excelled at; he served in both the North

Carolina and Virginia legislatures, although his legislative career lacked the kind of details attributed to his prowess with horses. Johnson excelled at providing strategy to jockeys, did not take losses easily and had a knack for picking winners, as well as for spouting wisdom such as, "There is nothing so good for the inside of a man as the outside of a horse" and, "Twixt the saddle and the ground, the sinner has Salvation found."

Horse racing was a congenial pastime, and the owners of the tracks considered races as opportunities to provide good hospitality, as well as betting. Racing enthusiasts enjoyed the good food and spirits offered by their hosts. Johnson liked to entertain the racing crowd, and he and Polly were known for their welcoming home, impeccable manners and unostentatious dress. Horse breeding was a profitable occupation as well, as the resulting offspring provided status and transportation. Wealthier patrons such as John Randolph often hurried home from their business in the nation's capital to see to their horses, and Randolph in particular owned 130 horses at the time of his death and was known to be a big gambler.

The year 1823 saw issues beginning to brew between North and South. Tensions were rising, and the North/South horse races, a series of thirty regional contests, epitomized the conflict. Traditionally, horse racing was a staple of southern culture, and southerners considered themselves superior owners and trainers, but in the course of the North/South races, the northern horses had been winning.

These famous races, called the intersectional match races, were depicted by Currier engravings and are said to have been the catalyst that sparked America's passionate interest in sporting events. With his winning record and unique skills, Johnson stepped into this situation, and his uncanny abilities were reported to have resulted in his followers winning an estimated $2 million during the North/South races. People got caught up in this regional competition, and in May 1825 some sixty thousand people gathered together with passion to watch the first major American sporting event at a racetrack in Long Island.

The famous race of May 1825 was instigated by Johnson's challenge of Eclipse, the horse of the North considered to be the greatest horse at the time. Congress was shut down and the stock exchange closed for this race, and even President Andrew Jackson attended the race at Union Course in Jamaica, New York. The horse pitted against Eclipse—Johnson's horse, called Sir Henry—was the son of Sir Archy.

The purse was $20,000, and the race consisted of three heats of four miles each, with thirty minutes between races. Legend has it that Johnson's overindulgence at dinner the night before caused him to be indisposed

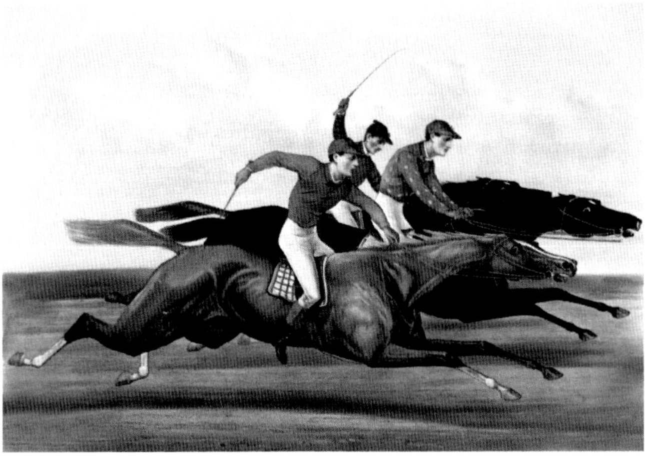

Currier and Ives, copyright 1884. "An Exciting Finish." *Library of Congress.*

during the race and thus unable to direct jockey strategy. Henry won the first heat in record time, and Eclipse took the second. Due to Johnson's absence from the track, no new jockey was mounted on Sir Henry for the final heat, and he lost the race.

In his middle age, Johnson turned his attention toward politics, until he retired in 1838. He continued to manage the southern side in the North/South races, but without the fervor of the early years. Upon his retirement from public service, he culled his racehorses down to just a few and, after a disappointing loss in 1842, left the intersectional races altogether. He reemerged for a final winning streak with a horse called Revenue, which won seven races in Louisiana in 1847 and 1848, before he died suddenly the following year at age sixty-seven.

William Ransom Johnson was buried at Oakland beside his wife, Polly. Inducted into the National Museum of Racing's Hall of Fame in 1986, Johnson is considered to have had such a glorious career in horse training and racing that his loss in 1825 was not significant to his legacy, but the chance "perfect storm" of food-caused illness, lack of organization behind the scenes and the unprecedented scale of the sporting event must have caused him many sleepless nights.

As for the horses, Diomed lived to be twenty-seven years old and was at stud for seven seasons. Sir Archy earned more than $79,000 in stud fees until his death in 1833. In the end, he was pulled from racing because no one would race or bet against him. The contenders in the great race, Eclipse and Sir Henry, changed residences in retirement. Eclipse was auctioned and then leased to a Virginian who later sold him to Johnson, and Sir Henry was put to stud in the North, where he went lame and was retired at age six.

Appendix
Notes on Sources

Lord Chesterfield was a prolific writer. Refer to the Library of Congress for a listing of his works (www.loc.gov).

The research library of the Chesterfield Historical Society of Virginia has old maps and vertical files (loose papers) that provide insight into the history of Chesterfield County.

The *Richmond News Leader*, *Richmond Times-Dispatch*, *Richmond Enquirer* and other old newspapers are part of the National Digital Newspaper Program and compose the Virginia Digital Newspaper Program (VaDNP). Visit www.loc.gov/rr/news or www.chroniclingamerica.loc.gov. Some newspapers are available on microfilm at the Library of Virginia, and some originals can be found at the Virginia Historical Society.

For more information on the Huguenots in Virginia, see the Huguenot Society of the Founders of Manakin in the Colony of Virginia at www.manakin.addr.com.

For more information on Civil War sites and sesquicentennial events in Chesterfield and throughout Virginia, visit www.virginiacivilwar.org.

The Officer Down Memorial Page, 1996, is found at www.odmp.org.2009.

The Hallsboro Store and the Hallsboro Tavern are listed on the National Register of Historic Places. See www.dhr.virginia.gov/registers/counties/chesterfield. The tavern is on the county and state registries.

The Stewart-Pocahontas Museum was created by Richard Stewart, resident historian and honorary mayor of Pocahontas Island. His museum is open "by appointment or by chance" and includes a wide array of historic documents, photographs, artifacts and memorabilia.

The Castlewood Historic Preservation Certification Application, architectural reports and landmark applications can be reviewed from the vertical files at the CHS library.

Hening's Statues at Large is the collection of all the laws of Virginia from 1619 to 1792. It was compiled by William Waller Hening.

Independent research by the CHS cemetery committee and by Mrs. Shirley Diller enabled us to get a good feel for what preceded Pocahontas State Park. These records are kept in the CHS library.

The minutes of the Chesterfield County School Board, on microfilm, can be reviewed in the Local History room at Central Library.

Bibliography

Carty, Kathleen Burris. *Matoaca, A "King Cotton" Village in Earlier Days.* N.p.: self-published, 2009.

Church, Randolph W. "Mr. Nellywood and the Querry Hole." *Virginia Cavalcade* magazine (Summer 1954): 5.

Dobree, Bonamy, ed. *The Letters of Lord Chesterfield in Six Volumes.* Vol. 1. New York: AMS Press, 1932.

Eisenberg, John. *The Great Match Race.* New York: Houghton Mifflin Company, 2006.

English, Beth. "'I…Have a Lot of Work to Do': Cotton Mill Work and Women's Culture in Matoaca, Virginia, 1888–1895." *Virginia Magazine of History and Biography* 114, no. 3, 357.

The Great Beattie Murder Case. Baltimore, MD: Phoenix Publishing Company, 1911.

Howe, Mary Ellen. *Richard Bailey.* Vol. 1. Petersburg, VA: M.E. Howe, 1984–2003.

Logan, Kate Virginia Cox. *My Confederate Girlhood.* Richmond, VA: Garrett & Massie, Inc., 1932.

Lutz, Francis Earle. *Chesterfield: An Old Virginia County.* Vol. 1. *1607–1954.* Richmond, VA: Chesterfield Museum Committee of the Chesterfield Historical Society, 1992.

O'Dell, Jeffrey M. *Chesterfield County: Early Architecture and Historic Sites.* Chesterfield, VA: Chesterfield County Planning Department, 1983.

Robins, Sally Nelson. *Love Stories of Famous Virginians.* 2nd ed. Richmond, VA: Dietz Printing Co., 1925.

Weaver, Bettie Woodson. *History and Geography of Chesterfield County, Virginia.* Chesterfield, VA: Chesterfield County Public Schools, 1981.

INDEX

About the Author

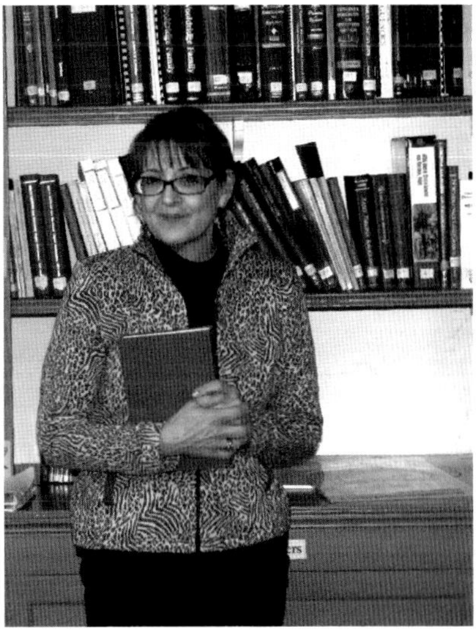

A recent convert to the lure of history, Diane Dallmeyer moved to Chesterfield County after elementary school. Coming from the Midwest, "I missed the elementary school lessons about our community," she writes, "so it took me a few more years to discover the many ways in which Chesterfield's story is so truly unique." After earning a Bachelor of Science degree in business at James Madison University, Diane returned to Chesterfield, where she has remained and raised her three sons. A career change brought her to the Chesterfield Historical Society, where she has enjoyed reusing the tools of writing sharpened in college by contributing articles to the *Chesterfield Observer*, some of which are contained in this book.